Cambridge E

Elements in P

edited by
James T. Enns
The University of British Columbia

REPRESENTING
VARIABILITY

*How Do We Process the
Heterogeneity in the Visual
Environment?*

Andrey Chetverikov
University of Bergen

Árni Kristjánsson
University of Iceland

CAMBRIDGE
UNIVERSITY PRESS

Shaftesbury Road, Cambridge CB2 8EA, United Kingdom

One Liberty Plaza, 20th Floor, New York, NY 10006, USA

477 Williamstown Road, Port Melbourne, VIC 3207, Australia

314–321, 3rd Floor, Plot 3, Splendor Forum, Jasola District Centre, New Delhi – 110025, India

103 Penang Road, #05–06/07, Visioncrest Commercial, Singapore 238467

Cambridge University Press is part of Cambridge University Press & Assessment, a department of the University of Cambridge.

We share the University's mission to contribute to society through the pursuit of education, learning and research at the highest international levels of excellence.

www.cambridge.org
Information on this title: www.cambridge.org/9781009478861

DOI: 10.1017/9781009396035

When citing this work, please include a reference to the DOI 10.1017/9781009396035

First published 2024

A catalogue record for this publication is available from the British Library.

ISBN 978-1-009-47886-1 Hardback
ISBN 978-1-009-39601-1 Paperback
ISSN 2515-0502 (online)
ISSN 2515-0499 (print)

Cambridge University Press & Assessment has no responsibility for the persistence or accuracy of URLs for external or third-party internet websites referred to in this publication and does not guarantee that any content on such websites is, or will remain, accurate or appropriate.

Representing Variability

How Do We Process the Heterogeneity in the Visual Environment?

Elements in Perception

DOI: 10.1017/9781009396035
First published online: February 2024

Andrey Chetverikov
University of Bergen

Árni Kristjánsson
University of Iceland

Author for correspondence: Andrey Chetverikov,
andrey.a.chetverikov@gmail.com

Abstract: The visual world is full of detail. This Element focuses on this variability in perception, asking how it affects performance in visual tasks and how the variability is represented by human observers. The authors highlight different methods for assessing representations of variability and suggest that understanding visual variability can be elusive when straightforward explicit methods are used, while more implicit methods may be better suited to uncovering such processing. The authors conclude that variability is represented in far more detail than previously thought and that this aspect of perception is vital for understanding the complexity of visual consciousness.

Keywords: variability perception, summary statistics, perceptual uncertainty, probabilistic brain, external noise

ISBNs: 9781009478861 (HB), 9781009396011 (PB), 9781009396035 (OC)
ISSNs: 2515-0502 (online), 2515-0499 (print)

Contents

1 Introduction

Since the publication of Fechner's 'Elements of Psychophysics' (1860), a major goal within vision science has been to build models of how the visual system operates in real-world scenarios from studies with simple stimuli in tightly controlled experimental settings. The last decade has seen an important shift in perspective away from this extreme reductionism, however: instead of focusing on stimuli that have only one feature value (e.g., a single hue or orientation), researchers have increasingly used heterogenous stimuli with features varying in space (e.g., an apple; Figure 1) and time (e.g., sequences of different colours) to understand how they are perceived and represented. This matches a recent general trend towards a focus on probabilistic models of perception and has provided exciting new insights about visual processing. Here we ask: how does information about such heterogeneous stimuli affect performance in visual tasks, and how is it acquired and represented?

1.1 Variability Is a Fundamental Aspect of How the Richness of the Environment Is Represented

One fundamental aspect of the real world is the enormous *variability* in the input. In this overview, our aim is to connect disparate threads of studies of visual variability in different domains (e.g., orientation, colour, shape) and at different timescales (from one-shot perception to long-term learning) to uncover how the visual system extracts the variability in the visual world and how it is represented.

The visual environment contains a lot of variability and notable detail. How are these visual stimuli and the variation within them represented? It seems fair to say that the basic assumption in the literature has been that single value estimates are the unit of, for example, attentional processing, working memory (Cohen et al., 2016), and so on, and that these single point representations can be noisy (Bays et al., 2022). But importantly a key assumption seems to be that the visual system does not make any attempt at actually representing the variability, as such.

It is indeed a popular view within the visual perception literature that we represent far less of the visual environment than we often feel we do. An often-cited example is how studies of change blindness and inattentional blindness seem to indicate that we represent much less of our visual environments than we think we do. This general idea comes in many flavours and has been called the 'grand illusion' view (O'Regan & Noë, 2001; Rensink, 2000; Simons, 2000). It is fundamentally important, however, to note that even if change blindness occurs, this does not *preclude* that detail is represented since there can certainly

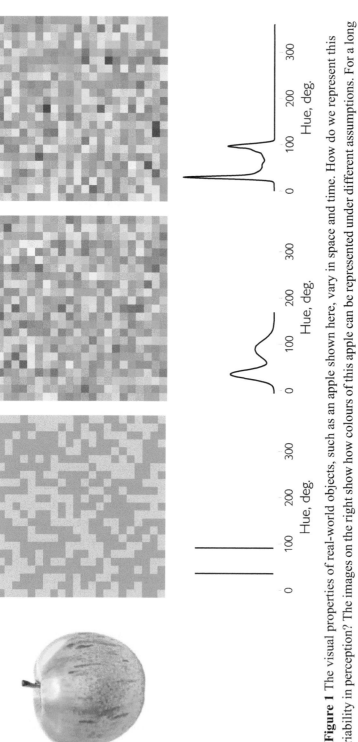

Figure 1 The visual properties of real-world objects, such as an apple shown here, vary in space and time. How do we represent this variability in perception? The images on the right show how colours of this apple can be represented under different assumptions. For a long time, studies in vision science mostly used stimuli with discrete non-varying features, as if the apple can be represented with just two colours (left). More recently, a summary statistics account has emerged that suggests that a few summary statistics (e.g., mean and variance) are enough to describe the visual variability (middle). But other studies indicate that visual representations can be more complex, taking into account the properties of visual features beyond simple statistics (right). Plots on the bottom show the probability distributions of the colours of the apple under these assumptions while the upper row shows colours randomly sampled from these distributions.

be a clear distinction between what can be consciously reported and what can be represented (Fernandez-Duque & Thornton, 2000; Haberman & Whitney, 2011; Hansmann-Roth et al., 2021; see Haun et al., 2017 for a recent discussion). One need not look further than the famous findings within neuropsychology, at phenomena such as blindsight or hemispatial neglect, to see clear examples of this.

1.2 Uncertainty as a Dimension in Perception

Recently, this trend for sparseness and summaries has been changing, however, with the increased popularity of probabilistic views of perception (Koblinger et al., 2021; Ma, 2012; Tanrıkulu et al., 2021a). Such probabilistic accounts of perception tend to assume that our brains perform probabilistic calculations involving uncertainty. Visual information is thought to be represented as a probability density function of potential feature values of visual items rather than as representation of a single value. In a recent article, Yoo et al. (2021) tested an orientation change detection task where one condition required the maintenance of the uncertainty in the stimulation while the other condition did not require this. Yoo et al. found that uncertainty is represented in working memory (rather than the representations simply being noisy). This result argues against single value accounts of working memory since the result indicated that it is not just that estimates are noisy, but uncertainty is actually represented. Consistent with this, variability can be primed, importantly, even when the features of the prime and target come from different categories (Michael et al., 2014).

It has indeed been suggested that variability operates as a separate dimension in visual processing (Norman et al., 2015). Norman et al. found that adaptation to variance in orientation caused a negative after-effect in the perceived variance. Importantly the adaptation was present across changes in mean orientation, which showed that the adaptation to variability applied independently of the actual mean orientation. Notably, this variability adaptation was retinotopic but not spatiotopic, presumably indicating processing at relatively early levels. What is interesting here, is how this suggests that variance can be considered a *special perceptual dimension*. The results of Norman et al. (2015) show how variation is an entity in orientation space that is not bound to its mean (but see Section 3.1.1 for contradicting results). The findings of Maule and Franklin (2020) also support the view that variance is a special dimension in perception. They found that adaptation to a high-variance colour ensemble led to a negative after-effect, where an orientation ensemble was judged to be less variable than it actually was. This highlights how variability alone can be important in what we perceive.

In what follows, we will review how the heterogeneity (or variability) of visual stimuli matters for different visual tasks, ranging from classic findings on the effects of distractor variability in visual search (Duncan & Humphreys, 1989) to recent reports on the role of variability in crowding (Tiurina et al., 2022). Having shown how heterogeneity can help or hinder performance on a variety of perceptual tasks, we will then discuss attempts at uncovering the details of how it is represented. We will cover various approaches to this problem, ranging from classical psychophysics (Dakin, 2001; Lau & Brady, 2018) and explicit reproduction (Oriet & Hozempa, 2016), to more implicit paradigms where representations are reconstructed from behavioural performance (e.g., Acerbi et al., 2012; Chetverikov et al., 2016, 2019; Hansmann-Roth et al., 2021, 2022; Tanrıkulu et al., 2021a).

One of our aims here is to argue against 'grand illusion' accounts of visual perception. Various authors have argued that our impression of a world that is rich, detailed and continuous over time is illusory. To the casual reader (and perceiver) such arguments may seem ludicrous, but there is interesting experimental evidence that does suggest that such views should at least be taken seriously. The most pertinent findings are, on the one hand, change blindness and inattentional blindness, and then a large amount of evidence for the processing of summary statistics in the visual input (Corbett et al., 2023; Haberman & Whitney, 2012). One of the main messages here is how research into how human observers represent variability reveals that far more detail is represented and processed than such accounts propose.

1.3 Clarifying the Definitions

When discussing variability and how it is represented, it is important to distinguish between the variability and the observers' internal representation of the variability, between explicit and implicit representations, and between variability representation and uncertainty. We will use the term *variability* to refer to variation in the features of stimuli in space and time. In particular, we will often talk about feature probability distributions, or *feature distributions*, for brevity. A probability distribution is a mathematical concept defining how probable each feature value is within a certain set of stimuli. The feature distribution is a characteristic of the visual world and is not directly available to observers, however, they might build a representation of it from incoming sensory signals.

Observers' representations of variability can be explicit or implicit (Figure 2). By explicit representation of variability, we mean a representation in which the amount of variability is represented as a parameter, for example, as a standard deviation or range of stimuli features. Such explicit representations are often parts of traditional Bayesian ideal observer models along with the mean or other parameters (e.g., van den Berg & Ma, 2012). Note that while we depict explicit representation of variance in Figure 2 as having uncertainty (see later in this section), it can also be represented as a fixed parameter or, if it is to be inferred, as a point estimate. In contrast, variability can also be represented *implicitly* as part of the representation of a feature distribution. That is, if an observer knows the probabilities of different feature values (not necessarily matching the feature distribution accurately), this knowledge will implicitly include knowledge about their variability even though no specific parameter describes the variability *per se*.

Implicit representations of variability can be, in turn, model-free or model-based. If the observer has an explicit representation of variability and other parameters, this model can be used to infer the probability of different features (a posterior predictive distribution in Bayesian terms), a model-based implicit representation of variability. On the other hand, a model-free representation can also emerge if sensory signals are used to directly infer the feature probabilities.

Uncertainty is different from variability, as the former term is used here and in the literature (e.g., Koblinger et al., 2021; Rahnev et al., 2021), to refer to the amount of information in the internal representation of some inferred quantity. Inferred is an important qualifier here as uncertainty arises only when an observer is trying to go beyond the data at hand. For example, if you need to compute the average height of four people, you can do so precisely and there will be no uncertainty. But if you are told that these people are randomly picked from some population and are asked to infer the average height in that population, there will be uncertainty in your estimate, and it will probably be quite high in this case, since your data set consists of only a tiny part of the population. This distinction is important because *estimates* of variability (e.g., variance or range) will have their own uncertainty. At the same time, as we will discuss in more detail later, variability can create uncertainty in other estimates (such as the average), but such uncertainty does not necessarily imply that variability is represented.

We will also distinguish between *summary statistics* and *image-computable statistics*. We will use the term 'summary statistics' to refer to summaries of visual features as, for example their mean, variance, range, or skew, such as when observers can relatively accurately infer the mean size or orientation of stimulus sets (Corbett et al., 2023; Haberman & Whitney, 2012). The outputs from multi-level image processing filters (Balas et al., 2009; Freeman & Simoncelli, 2011; Portilla & Simoncelli, 2000) are also sometimes referred to as summary statistics but they are a far more complex entity, so to avoid confusion, we will refer to them as image-computable statistics (see Rosenholtz, 2020 for a more detailed discussion of this distinction).

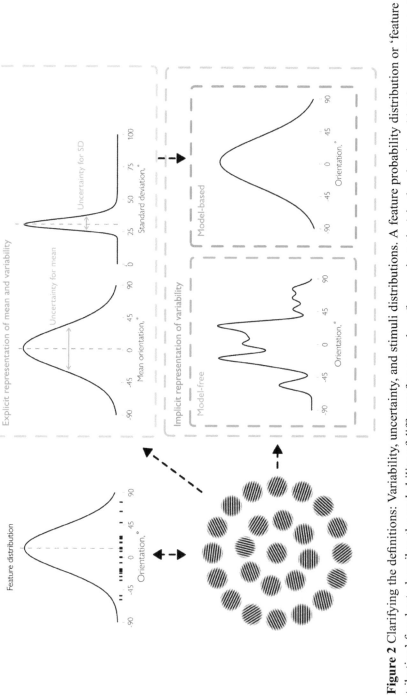

Figure 2 Clarifying the definitions: Variability, uncertainty, and stimuli distributions. A feature probability distribution or 'feature distribution' for short, describes the probability of different feature values (here, orientation) in the visual world. It is unavailable to the observer in any direct way. The observer can then represent the variability of stimuli (here, orientations of Gabor patches) in different ways.

Caption for Figure 2 (cont.)

First, following the traditional Bayesian ideal observer approach, the observer can use a certain model to represent or estimate the environmental statistics, including, for example, the mean and a variability-related quantity (e.g., standard deviation). In this case, the variability (along with the mean) could be said to be represented explicitly. This is different from the representation of uncertainty often discussed in the literature since uncertainty would correspond to the amount of information about the parameters (so there's uncertainty for the mean and the standard deviation). Alternatively, or perhaps in addition, the observer could use an implicit representation of variability incorporated into the estimated probability of occurrence of certain stimuli in the world, or essentially, an internal representation of a feature probability distribution. This implicit representation does not have a parameter (like variance in the other version) for variability and is hence implicit. But it can be either model-free or model-based, with the model-based representation based on a model, such as the one discussed in Section 1.3.

2 How Does Variability Affect Visual Cognition?

2.1 Visual Search

Does variability matter for visual perception? One of the fields within vision science where this question has been thoroughly explored is visual search. In the most common version of the visual search task, observers have to find a stimulus ('target') determined by a feature, such as colour or orientation, or a combination of features, among several 'distractors'. In a now classic study, Duncan and Humphreys (1989) found that people made fewer mistakes when distractors were identical to each other compared to when they varied. In Driver et al. (1992), visual search performance was modulated by whether the search items oscillated in phase with one another or not. Search was most difficult when the search items that moved in the motion direction that denoted the target, moved out of phase with each other and the items moving in the nontarget direction also moved out of phase with each other, therefore increasing variability. Later, Nagy et al. (2005) tested search for targets defined by colour and found that when the colour values of the stimuli were varied on another cardinal axis than the cardinal axis which differentiated the targets from distractors, visual search was also impaired. Generally, the effect of distractor variability has then been replicated in many studies for various feature dimensions (e.g., Avraham et al., 2008; Calder-Travis & Ma, 2020; Chetverikov et al., 2016; Mazyar et al., 2013; Rosenholtz, 2001; Utochkin, 2013; Vincent et al., 2009).

Notably, however, high distractor variability is not always detrimental to performance. Duncan and Humphreys (1989) suggested that the effect of distractor variability depends on target-distractor similarity (and vice versa). More specifically, they suggested that when distractors are very dissimilar from the target, increasing their heterogeneity should have little or no effects on performance. In contrast, when distractors become more similar to targets, search performance should become worse with increasing heterogeneity. This prediction has been found to hold in studies where the effects of distractor variability upon visual search performance were weaker as the distractors became more dissimilar to targets (Calder-Travis & Ma, 2020; Chetverikov et al., 2016; Rosenholtz, 2001).

While distractor heterogeneity clearly affects performance, some recent studies suggest that it is not the heterogeneity of distractors *per se*, but instead, what might be called its side effects, that are important. Calder-Travis and Ma (2020) and Mihali and Ma (2020) noted that since increasing distractor variability increases the range of distractor features, the distance between a target and the distractor most similar to it becomes lower. They further showed that when both factors are taken into account, it is the minimal distance and not the variability that has the strongest effect on performance. Others, however, have found effects of distractor variability even when the minimum target to distractor similarity is controlled for (Chetverikov et al., 2016; Rosenholtz, 2001). Rosenholtz (2001) also reported that the denser the displays, the larger the effect of variability.

Can distractor variability be beneficial for visual search? Interestingly, Utochkin and Yurevich (2016) tested an orientation search task, finding that search became more difficult with three distinct groups of distractors (e.g., a third of stimuli oriented at 45 deg., a third at 67.5 deg., and a third at 90 deg.) than search with two groups within the same range of orientations (e.g., half of the distractors at 45 deg. and half at 90 deg.), even though the standard deviation of distractors was higher in the latter case than in the former. They explained the findings by introducing the concept of 'segmentability', suggesting that observers automatically group (or 'segment') distractors into subsets, so that performance is better when distractors are more variable but easier to group together (see also Duncan & Humphreys, 1989; Wang et al., 2005). Similar patterns of results have also been observed in ensemble averaging studies (see Section 2.3) and this raises interesting questions about the meaning of variability in the light of the hierarchical nature of visual information processing.

2.2 Crowding

Crowding refers to impaired identification of object features when an object, usually in the periphery of the visual field, is presented in a particular context, such as among one or several flanking items (Whitney & Levi, 2011). Crowding occurs when objects that are easily recognized and visible in isolation become unrecognizable when they are viewed in clutter.

The effects of variability upon crowding can be seen when the visibility of a stimulus is affected. Increasing flanker heterogeneity usually increases crowding strength (Põder, 2012). Interestingly, in the so-called uncrowding effect, adding several identical flankers may reduce the strength of crowding compared to one flanker, but making them more heterogeneous re-establishes the crowding power of the flankers (Manassi et al., 2016). Tiurina et al. (2022) have recently shown that this effect also depends on the similarity of the key flanking element around the target to other flankers. They found that when all other parameters are kept constant, increasing the heterogeneity of other flankers makes crowding stronger in line with earlier reports. But the effect of variability was only observed when the key flanker matched the average of the other flanker features. When the key flanker was distinct from the additional flankers, the size of crowding effects was at the same high level as when no additional flankers were introduced, irrespective of variability. This suggests that variability effects in crowding can be moderated by the similarity between flankers, and, potentially, between targets and flankers, but again shows a clear effect of variability.

2.3 Perceptual Averaging

The effects of variability have been studied extensively in the context of perceptual averaging, which involves the ability to aggregate information from multiple stimuli to estimate their average properties (see Bauer, 2015; Corbett et al., 2023; Whitney & Yamanashi Leib, 2018, for reviews). Usually, heterogeneity in the stimuli set is detrimental to averaging (e.g., Bertana et al., 2021; Dakin, 2001; Im & Halberda, 2013; Li et al., 2017; Maule & Franklin, 2015; Sama et al., 2021; Semizer & Boduroglu, 2021; Solomon, 2010; Utochkin & Tiurina, 2014; see Hochstein et al., 2018; Lau & Brady, 2018, for exceptions). This is indeed to be expected if observers are trying to infer the stimuli from noisy sensory samples, because the standard error of the mean is a function of population variance and sample size. Variability in the stimuli must then affect mean estimation performance.

Like in other cases, the effects of variability can be observed at multiple levels of the visual hierarchy. That is, the number of stimulus subsets or the ease with which they can be grouped is an important factor in determining the averaging performance (Attarha et al., 2014; Attarha & Moore, 2015; Im et al., 2020; Tiurina et al., 2022). For example, in Attarha and Moore (2015) four clusters of several circles of varied size appeared around a fixation point and the task of the observers was to find either the cluster with the smallest or largest mean size. Attarha and Moore found an advantage for the judgments when they could be performed simultaneously rather than sequentially, which argues for a fixed processing capacity for multiple ensembles, but also that the processing capacity for a single ensemble is virtually unlimited.

2.4 Visual Working Memory

How are working memory capacity and performance affected by variability? If there is a single object with varying elements to be remembered, then working memory tasks can effectively turn into averaging tasks, if observers attempt to keep an average representation of the stimulus set in mind. As discussed Section 2.3, averaging performance depends on variability. But interestingly, working memory is also affected by stimulus variability in multi-stimulus displays when only a single stimulus has to be reported. Utochkin and Brady (2020) used a standard working memory task with four elements that had a varying range of orientations. They found that for displays with a relatively narrow range of orientations, observers remembered individual elements with higher precision than when the range was wider. This finding is in line with the hierarchical model of working memory (Brady & Alvarez, 2011; Haberman et al., 2015a) which suggests that observers encode the properties of the whole stimulus set along with the individual items and both are combined in memory reports. Since higher between-stimuli variability decreases the precision of mean estimates (as discussed in Section 2.3 and replicated by Utochkin & Brady, 2020), the precision of reports for individual items drops as well. So even when there is no variability at the level of individual stimuli, the variability of the stimulus set nevertheless affects working memory performance for these individual stimuli.

2.5 Contextual Influences

In line with the working memory studies described in Section 2.4, variability also affects performance in tasks when the context is variable while the target stimulus is not. Li et al. (2018) demonstrated this in a version of a flanker task, where observers had to judge if the orientation of a central target surrounded by distractors was clockwise or counterclockwise. When the distractors were congruent with the target and had the same orientation (e.g., both were oriented at 45 deg.), response times were usually faster than when distractors had an orthogonal orientation (e.g., the target was at 45 deg. and distractors were at –45 deg.). This congruency effect is diminished when distractors have higher variability. However, congruent distractors can also hinder responses if the target is close to the decision boundary and distractors are further away from it. This effect is also diminished when variability in distractor orientations is introduced, making increased variability beneficial for performance.

2.6 Meta-cognition

Variability in the stimuli is also an important meta-cognitive cue to inform observers' own judgments about their perceptual performance, such as when observers are asked to decide how confident they are about a decision (Bertana et al., 2021; Boldt et al., 2017; Gao et al., 2023; Spence et al., 2016, 2018; Zylberberg et al., 2014). Usually, confidence is positively correlated with performance (e.g., Pleskac & Busemeyer, 2010), so when observers' performance becomes worse due to increased variability in the stimuli, their confidence about their performance tends to decrease as well. Notably, however, effects of variability on confidence have often been observed even when performance is unaffected. For example, Zylberberg et al. (2014) used a motion discrimination task with randomly moving dots. The distance to the decision boundary (e.g., 90 deg. when observers had to decide whether dots were moving in the clockwise or counterclockwise directions) and variability in the dot motion directions in this task both affected performance and could be manipulated independently. This is important since it allows the dissociation of objective performance from variability through manipulation of the distance to the decision boundary. Zylberberg and colleagues found that when objective performance levels are kept the same, confidence nevertheless decreases with increasing variability, highlighting that the effect of variability on confidence is not only due to differences in performance, and lent support to the view of a special status for variability in visual perception.

But the opposite relationship between variability and performance and variability and confidence can also be demonstrated. For example, Gao and colleagues (2023) manipulated variability in the direction of moving dots while asking observers to judge if the majority of dots were moving to the left or right. Importantly, confidence about performance was higher while the performance itself was worse when the overall proportion of dots moving in the target direction was increased. This is because the authors increased not just the proportion of dots moving in the target direction but also the proportion of dots moving in the opposite direction among randomly moving dots. They argued that this manipulation increases noise in sensory signals which can lead to very strong signals which then results in higher confidence. For discrimination performance, on the other hand, the ratio of the dots moving in the true and the opposite direction might be more important as it could determine the discriminability of sensory signals in a signal-detection theoretic model (but note that the presence of orientation signals in motion direction might make the explanation of these findings more complex, see Chetverikov & Jehee, 2023). In sum, these results suggest that variability might have opposing effects on confidence about performance, and performance itself, making it important to model the effects of variability in computational models, to obtain precise predictions about performance.

In other studies, meta-cognition (measured by confidence ratings) does not seem to be particularly sensitive enough to the changes in variability. For example, Herce Castañón et al. (2019) tested participants in three conditions on a 2AFC orientation discrimination task with arrays of Gabor patches presented on each trial. Compared to a *baseline* condition, both low contrast and high variability had similar detrimental effects on performance. However, overconfidence (measured as the difference between mean binary confidence and mean choice accuracy) was higher in the high variability condition than in the low contrast condition.

Another important observation is that it is the *perceived* variability rather than the actual variation of stimulus features that seems to play a major role in this context. Bertana and colleagues (2021) found that, paradoxically, in an orientation averaging task, objective performance deteriorates but confidence increases from cardinal (i.e., 0 or 90 deg.) to oblique (45 or 135 deg.) orientations. The decrease in objective performance from cardinal to oblique orientations is well known in the literature as the 'oblique effect' and is usually explained by the tuning of the visual system to the statistics of the visual world, where cardinal orientations are overrepresented (Girshick et al., 2011). In other words, the internal noise of the visual system is lower for cardinal than for oblique orientations. But why does the confidence increase for oblique orientations? Bertana et al. demonstrated that this increase in confidence is related to the fact that it is easier to perceive variability in the stimulus (or, alternatively, more noise is perceived) when internal noise is low. Hence, while the task becomes more difficult for observers on trials with more oblique orientations, these same observers also underestimate the amount of variability, which, in turn, leads to higher confidence about the judgments. This surprising finding demonstrates the importance of perceived variability for metacognition.

2.7 Perceptual Learning

Are there effects of variability upon perceptual learning? Perceptual learning has been considered unique in the literature, in that it has typically been found to be retinotopic (or location specific) and also specific to the particular stimuli that observers are trained on. Such specificity may make perceptual learning less useful than it could be (Fahle, 2005). However, there is evidence that variability in stimulation can aid the generalizability of perceptual learning. Manenti et al. (2023) tested whether introducing variability in stimulation can 'unlock' generalizability in perceptual learning. While their subjects were trained on an orientation task, variability on an irrelevant feature (spatial frequency) was introduced. This manipulation led to generalization to other locations and stimuli while the perceptual learning itself was unaffected. Similarly, Hussain et al. (2012) tested perceptual learning of textures, finding that the learning was specific, suffering when textures were rotated or changed in polarity, for observers who had trained on the same ten standard stimuli. But for groups whose learning had proceeded on more variable sets of stimuli, performance was not affected. This shows how perceptual learning is adaptable and can generalize, and that variability can aid with this. Hussain and colleagues argued that 'increasing stimulus variability by reducing the number of times stimuli are repeated during practice may cause subjects to adopt strategies that increase generalization of learning to new stimuli' (p. 89). Other forms of learning might benefit from variability as well. For example, Higuchi et al. (2020) found that contextual cueing (which involves visual search with a consistent association between the target and distractor locations that observers learn over trials) can also benefit from variability in stimuli locations. Corpuz and Oriet (2022) then demonstrated that variability can also be helpful in learning facial identities. Overall, the more varied the input, the longer the learning takes, but the benefit of this increased variability seems to be that the learning becomes more general (Raviv et al., 2022).

2.8 Summary

The overview in Sections 2.1–2.7 illustrates how variability within groups of stimuli strongly affects performance in a variety of cognitive and visual tasks. Many studies show how higher variability is generally detrimental to performance, although it can become beneficial under certain specific circumstances. On the one hand, this is clearly expected and can be seen as an effect reflecting the signal to noise ratio in the stimuli. When observers have to combine information from multiple stimuli (e.g., estimate their mean feature value or other properties needed for a given task), variability increases the noise, resulting in a negative effect on performance. On the other hand, noise in irrelevant distracting information can reduce its effects on performance, which can sometimes be helpful as can be seen in flanker interference (Li et al., 2018).

The first notable caveat is that we show in Sections 2.1–2.7, variability must be considered at different levels of the information processing hierarchy. Higher variability at the level of individual stimulus features might mean that they will tend to be grouped together, leading to lower variability at the level of clusters or groups of stimuli. Secondly, as shown by Bertana et al. (2021), *perceived* variability might be more important than actual variability, at least for metacognition. While it is reasonable to suspect that perceived variability (rather than actual variability) might be important for other tasks as well, especially for grouping, to our best knowledge, this line of research has not been explored yet. Lastly, the effects of variability might be observed even if the stimulus itself does not vary while the context varies, even when the context is irrelevant to the main task that observers have to perform. This has been observed in working memory studies (Utochkin & Brady, 2020) and flanker tasks (Li et al., 2018). In summary, variability adds noise, which is often, but importantly not always, detrimental to the performance.

3 How Is Variability Represented?

An important consideration is that even if variability affects perceptual performance, that does not necessarily mean that the information about variability is represented anywhere in the visual system. While this might seem counterintuitive, averaging tasks can provide a clear example of why this is the case. If a participant is, for example, asked to compute the average colour from a set of colour patches, one viable strategy could be to sample one or several patches and then average their colours. If all the patches have the same hue, the task is very easy and can be performed by selecting just one patch. If they have different colours, this single stimulus strategy will now introduce an error even if the participant does not keep track of how variable the colours are. Here, variability therefore affects performance, and larger variability would in this case lead to poorer performance without any explicit representation of variability since the observer here just selects one (or multiple) patches. This is similar to the well-known difference between noise and uncertainty in the classic Bayesian perception literature (see, e.g., Ma, 2019), with the exception that variability representation does not necessarily mean uncertainty representation (see Section 1.3). So while variability affects performance in visual tasks, is it also represented, and if so, how?

Demonstrating that variability is represented, however, is not a simple task because in many cases (as we show in the following sections) there could be alternative ways of explaining empirical findings without presupposing explicit representations of variability. And in fact, within the field of vision science, it has been proposed that variability is not represented in detail, but instead only as summaries (Alvarez, 2011) and that any feeling that we may have for such detailed representations is illusory (Cohen et al., 2016; Noe et al., 2000; Rensink, 2000). In the following, we will discuss the approaches that have been used to test to what degree observers keep track of variability in the visual world (Figure 3).

3.1 Testing Variability Representations Explicitly

3.1.1 Forced-Choice Comparisons

Psychophysics has for a long time been a gold standard in vision science. By using forced-choice tasks in particular, one can show that observers are sensitive to diminutive changes in visual stimulation, for example, whether or not a single photon hits their retina (Hecht et al., 1942; Tinsley et al., 2016). Using diverse psychophysical approaches, through mostly forced-choice comparisons, many studies have demonstrated that observers can discriminate between

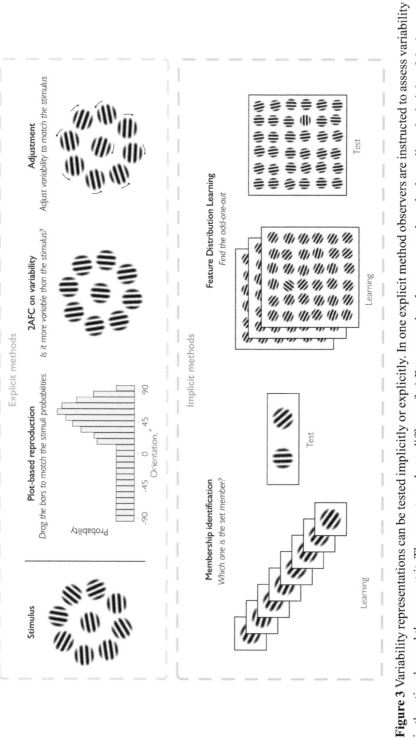

Figure 3 Variability representations can be tested implicitly or explicitly. In one explicit method observers are instructed to assess variability in the stimulus and then report it. The report can have different for) For example, observers can be asked to adjust the height of the bars on

Caption for Figure 3 (cont.)

a histogram to match the frequency or the probability of different feature values (see, e.g., Oriet & Hozempa, 2016). Alternatively, more classic psychophysical methods such as 2AFC or adjustment tasks can be used. In 2AFC tasks, observers are asked to compare the variability of the target stimulus with an alternative. In the adjustment task, observers adjust the variability of the stimulus (e.g., stimuli clockwise to the mean would be rotated one way, and stimuli counterclockwise to the mean would be rotated in the opposite way, increasing or decreasing the variability of the set as a whole). Implicit methods, on the other hand, do not instruct observers to assess variability, assuming instead that the variability is automatically picked up during the course of the task. For example, in the membership identification task (see, e.g., Khayat & Hochstein, 2018) observers first see a sequence of stimuli and are then asked to determine which of the two test stimuli belongs to the set they saw. Variability of the set would affect the judgments of the test stimuli even though observers are not asked to assess variability. The Feature Distribution Learning method (Chetverikov et al., 2016) uses a visual search task instead. During several learning trials, observers are asked to find the odd-one-out target among the set of distractors. Unbeknownst to them, distractors on each trial are randomly drawn from the same feature probability distribution. Then, on a test trial, the response times to a target as a function of its similarity to the previously learned distractor distribution, are used to infer how this distribution is represented. See detailed description of the different methods in the main text.

sets of stimuli differing in their variability (e.g., Atchley & Andersen, 1995; Cha et al., 2022, 2022; Dakin, 2001; Hansmann-Roth et al., 2021; Harrison et al., 2021; Lathrop, 1967; Lau & Brady, 2018; Morgan et al., 2008; Tokita et al., 2016; see Bauer, 2015; Corbett et al., 2023; Whitney & Yamanashi Leib, 2018 for reviews). The fact that observers can discriminate the variability of stimulus sets necessarily implies that variability is represented in some way. Unlike other tasks where variability could affect performance without being represented, it is impossible to compare variability itself among sets without representing it to some extent. For example, sampling just one item from each set would not allow any comparison of variability, and sampling two items and computing the differences within each set would result in a primitive range-based representation. It can be conscious or unconscious, but *something* is retained. How exactly is it represented? To answer this question, hypotheses can be tested about observers' performance in forced-choice comparisons under different assumptions about representations of variability.

For example, several studies have addressed whether information about variability is represented independently from information about the mean of the visual feature (Jeong & Chong, 2020; Maule & Franklin, 2020; Norman et al., 2015; Tong et al., 2015; Ueda et al., 2023). The question, in other words, is whether there are separate representations of variability as a summary statistic of some kind or whether this is closer to a representation of a probability distribution of visual features, where different parameters such as the mean or variance are bound together? The results on this are unfortunately inconclusive, so far. Norman et al. (2015) and Maule and Franklin (2020) found that after adaptation to an ensemble with a given variability in hue or orientation, observers are biased when they have to perform a variability discrimination task. This happens even when the mean of the feature is varied randomly (Maule & Franklin, 2020; Norman et al., 2015) or is orthogonal between the adaptor and the test stimulus (Norman et al., 2015). Interestingly, there is even evidence for adaptation across visual feature domains (from orientation to colour and vice versa, Maule & Franklin, 2020) and some limited evidence for adaptation effects between auditory and visual variability (Ueda et al., 2023). If the adaptation to variability has effects regardless of the mean or feature, this may reflect that the variability is represented separately from the mean, at least at some stage of processing. However, Jeong and Chong (2020) found that the adaptation to the mean orientation affects variance when the mean of the adapter and the test orientation are similar (presumably due to tilt after-effects) but not when the means are orthogonal. At the same time, they found that adaptation to ensembles with high or low variance affected the sensitivity of mean discrimination. These results suggest that mean and variance statistics are at least to some extent interrelated. Similarly, Tong et al. (2015) found that the discrimination of brightness variance is impaired when stimuli have different mean brightness. More research in this direction is therefore required to test whether variance is represented separately from the mean in a general sense, or if this only happens under some specific circumstances.

Lau and Brady (2018) suggested that the range heuristic, where the range (i.e., the difference between minimal and maximal values) is used as a heuristic proxy for variability, plays an important role in judgments of variability. The range is usually increased when variability is increased, and Lau and Brady postulated that range might be easier to compute than variance because it only requires finding the minimum and the maximum (although note that algorithmically finding the range is almost as complex as finding the variance, as both require iterating through all the items in a set once). They asked observers to determine which of two briefly presented sets of circles had higher size variability. On each trial, the sets differed in the variability and range of the sizes of the stimuli. When the two statistics were congruent (i.e., one set had a higher range *and* a higher variance), the observers more often selected the ensemble with higher variance than when they were incongruent. This suggests that people utilize both range and variance when asked to discriminate stimuli based on variability, potentially representing both measures during the decision-making process.

Jeong and Chong (2021) suggested that reliance on both the range and variance in variability estimates can be ascribed to variance-based estimates that account for item reliability. For example, outlying items can be automatically discarded in variability computations as not belonging to the same stimulus and items having higher contrast might be prioritized (see also findings on amplification in summary statistics judgments Iakovlev & Utochkin, 2021; Kanaya et al., 2018). From this perspective, incongruent stimuli pairs in Lau and Brady (2018) might result in poorer perceptual performance since the answer is counted as correct or not based on variance while observers actually use weighted variance to perform the task. More broadly, however, this highlights the difficulty of going beyond the 'can observers discriminate stimuli based on variability' question with classic psychophysics. The reason is that the answer in the variability discrimination task depends on the meaning observers apply to it. Answering this question might, therefore, be better suited to more implicit tasks than direct, explicit report tasks (see Section 3.2).

3.1.2 Adjustment Tasks

An alternative to forced-choice tests, also widely used in psychophysics, is the adjustment task. In such tasks, observers are asked to adjust the variability of a test set to match the variability of previously presented stimuli (Haberman et al., 2015b; Khvostov & Utochkin, 2019; Tokita et al., 2020). This method is seldom used, however, presumably because of the difficulties with manipulating the variability in an adjustment procedure (it is not clear how to change individual items when the variability of the set is to be increased or decreased). One approach is to shift each stimulus of the set by some amount in the feature space away or towards the mean (Figure 3).

Nevertheless, studies using this method have demonstrated that observers can successfully match the statistics of a comparison set, such as the range or variance of the set. Interestingly, Tokita et al. (2020) provided preliminary evidence that variability estimates for one dimension (e.g., size) can be reproduced by adjusting the variance in another dimension (e.g., orientation). This aligns well with data from studies where variance was estimated on a rating scale (Payzan-LeNestour et al., 2016; Suárez-Pinilla et al., 2018) and these results suggest, once again, that people can have an abstract representation of variability, or in other words that variability can be represented independently of any single particular stimulus dimension.

3.1.3 Explicit Reproduction of Distributions

Perhaps, the most straightforward way of assessing how variability is estimated is simply to ask observers to reproduce their impression of the variability within a set of stimuli. Ideally, such a procedure would involve an actual reproduction, for example, by drawing, or painting, a copy of an ensemble. However, this is obviously not only technically challenging, but also difficult in terms of a suitable measurement task, and, to our best knowledge, has not yet been done. Oriet and Hozempa (2016) used a related approach, where participants were asked to create a histogram of sizes for stimuli they saw by adjusting the height of the bars on a plot shown on the screen. They found that observers were quite inaccurate on this task, incorrectly reporting the range and the central tendency parameters of ensembles. For example, observers often indicated that stimuli included circles with very small sizes that were not present in the actual display. At the same time, when the displays had higher variability, the reproduced distributions also had higher variability, and observers were able to reproduce the skew in the displays as well.

Tran et al. (2017) have also demonstrated that it is difficult to explicitly reproduce a probability distribution when the learning of the statistics occurs over extended periods of time. Participants performed a computerized whack-a-mole game for 180 trials and were then asked to reproduce the distribution of the locations where the items to 'whack' appeared. The tested distributions were in some cases bimodal, and the only case where there was any remote evidence of the learning of bimodal distributions was when the bimodality was extreme, with zero probability density (or no exemplars) at the mean. Otherwise, the reproductions showed no evidence of any learning of distribution shape. This suggests that only strong and clearly noticeable patterns occurring over longer time periods become explicitly registered and represented by observers.

As also noted by Oriet and Hozempa (2016, p. 10), explicit reproduction is a considerably complex task and it requires a lot of effort from participants. They have to first transform their visual representations into frequency distributions and then report them by transforming these frequencies into the responses in terms of histogram bar lengths (or the number of clicks on different locations in Tran et al., 2017). Such a double transformation might introduce substantial noise and biases in the reports, making the results difficult to interpret. But are there other possibilities than testing explicit reports of variability and distribution characteristics? One example of such a task is the recently developed feature distribution learning method (Chetverikov et al., 2016, 2017a, 2019; Chetverikov & Kristjánsson, 2022).

3.2 The Feature Distribution Learning Method and Other Implicit Approaches

Given the limitations of explicit tests discussed in Section 3.1, what other options are available to assess the internal representation of stimuli variability? Several approaches have been developed to assess representations of variability from behavioural responses without explicitly requiring observers to report (e.g., discriminate or estimate) variability (Acerbi et al., 2012; Chetverikov et al., 2016; Sama et al., 2021). Such implicit tests assume that observers have an internal model of variability in the stimulus and use it to guide their interactions with heterogeneity in the environment. The assumption is that such models can then be inferred by observing responses to different varieties of heterogeneous stimulus ensembles.

We will, in particular, highlight an exciting new method, *feature distribution learning* (FDL, Figure 4), introduced in Chetverikov et al. (2016) that is designed to address the question of how variability is represented (see Chetverikov et al., 2019 for a tutorial of the method). Chetverikov et al. started with the question of whether variability is represented only as summaries (such as the mean, and then variance or range). Or is more information represented than argued by advocates of the view that the detail we think we perceive in the environment is mostly illusory (e.g., Cohen et al., 2016; O'Regan & Noë, 2001)?

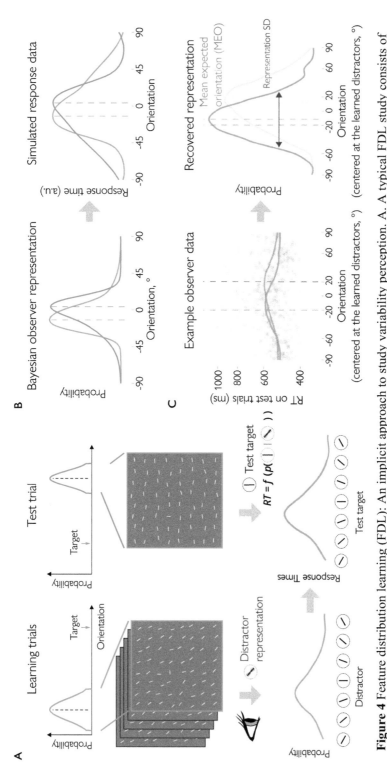

Figure 4 Feature distribution learning (FDL): An implicit approach to study variability perception. A. A typical FDL study consists of intermixed learning and test trials. Observers search for an odd-one-out target among a set of distractors. On learning trials, distractors are

Caption for Figure 4 (cont.)

randomly drawn from the same probability distribution on each trial while the target varies randomly with the important constraint that it remains dissimilar to distractors. The observers' performance quickly improves through the formation of a representation of distractors (bottom-left). On test trials, their knowledge of distractors is put to a test by introducing a target that can be more or less similar to previous distractors. B. Computational modelling (in Chetverikov & Kristjánsson, 2022) shows that for an ideal observer, the response times on test trials should be monotonically related to the expected probability of encountering a distractor with an orientation matching the test target, or in other words, distractor representations determine the response times. C. The relationship between representations and response times enables the recovery of the former from the latter. By collecting the data over many trials (dots in the left plot), the average response time curves (lines in the left plot) are transformed to obtain probability distributions corresponding to distractors (right plot). In addition to the overall shape of the distribution, their parameters such as the mean expected orientation and representation SD can then be analysed. This figure is based on Figures 1 and 2 from Chetverikov & Kristjánsson (2022) provided under CCBY-4.0 license.

The feature distribution learning method takes a novel approach to studying how representations of visual ensembles are formed. Rather than asking observes explicitly which ensemble has a higher mean, variance and so on, the representations are assessed indirectly and implicitly through effects upon response times and accuracy during visual search tasks. When observers have to respond to an unexpected target (such as when they have previously learned that the current target belongs within the range of possible distractors) their responses are slowed considerably (Chetverikov & Kristjánsson, 2015; Kristjánsson & Driver, 2008; Lamy et al., 2008; Wang et al., 2005). Importantly, this approach can reveal observers' learned representations of environmental statistics (Chetverikov et al., 2019).

3.2.1 Learning the Variability within the Visual World

When we open our eyes, it can take a while for us to understand our visual environment. While the basic details are available, various other nuances may take longer to make sense of. A good example is when you look down at a stream from a bridge. Someone tells you that there are small fish swimming all over the place in the stream, but you do not see any fish no matter how hard you try. But then suddenly you see a fish, and at that point, you can easily see that the fish is all over the place in the stream, akin to a phenomenon sometimes called 'perceptual insight' (e.g., Rubin et al., 1997). This is an example of how we can learn the statistics of the environment. Another example could be when we are assembling a jigsaw puzzle, over time and repeated exposure to the statistics within the image that we are assembling, we gradually learn where pieces with particular characteristics are likely to belong, a task that seemed almost impossible when we started assembling the puzzle – again, we learn the key statistics of such visual tasks over time. We learn over time that the patch of grass that seemed uniform, tends to have some positional nuances in feature values at a closer look.

Improved perception over time has been investigated in the perceptual learning literature, where experience-dependent improvements in our ability to make sense of what we see have been demonstrated (Gold & Watanabe, 2010). This training-induced perceptual learning (Seitz & Watanabe, 2005) can involve longer-term changes in perception (Karni & Sagi, 1991), even involving demonstrable changes at the neural level (Schwartz et al., 2002). But there is also an adjustment to the environment on shorter timescales, that is more fleeting and opportunistic and is more easily overridden by new input. Recent evidence where the feature distribution learning method has been used has revealed how this can occur (see review in Chetverikov et al., 2017a).

The feature distribution learning method relies on a simple principle: As we learn the characteristics of the environment, we come to expect certain basic properties that reflect these regularities. When our expectations are violated, this interferes with visual and attentional processing and this interference can cause measurable changes in behaviour – such as slowed processing of certain stimuli or decreased accuracy.

Let's say that you are picking blueberries. Over time you adjust your berry collecting (or 'foraging') to the mean and range of the colour variation of the ripe berries and at the same time learn the colours of what are *not* your targets (green leaves and nonripe green berries). Just as in the example with the fish in the stream, in Section 3.2.1, your visual system becomes better (or gains expertise, at least in the short term) at performing this task, despite large variations in lighting, shadows or reflection that can differently affect the actual reflectance and colour values of individual berries (Kristjánsson, 2022).

Analogies of such scenarios can be generated with computer displays involving tasks where observers are asked to find the oddly coloured item, for example. Once the participants have learned the properties of the environment, what happens when these properties are suddenly changed? Let's say that after searching for blue among green (as in the berry example in the previous paragraph), you are suddenly supposed to search for a green target within an environment that is made up of stimuli having various shades of blue instead of green. The FDL method relies on the fact that your representation of the learned environment can be assessed by how strongly your visual search performance is affected by this sudden change in the environment. These effects have been called role-reversal effects, in that a target of your search becomes part of the information that you are supposed to ignore, and vice versa, relying on findings from the literature on priming of attention shifts where when a target feature over a sequence of trials suddenly becomes the feature to ignore (the distractor colour, Chetverikov & Kristjánsson, 2015; Kristjánsson & Driver, 2008; see for example Kristjánsson & Ásgeirsson, 2019; Nakayama et al., 2004; Failing & Theeuwes, 2018 for review and see also Ramgir & Lamy, 2022 for some alternative views on priming in visual search).

The key point is that the green colours (or leaves of the berry bush, if we continue with the berry-picking analogy) have a distribution, they have a mean value, and a variance, but even more importantly, they may have distributions with various properties. Most of the leaves may have a relatively similar shade of green while a few may have started turning yellow, resulting in a colour distribution that is skewed towards yellow but has a mean at green. The key aspect of the FDL method is that the interference effect from the role-reversals (measured in response times) is sensitive to the distribution that you have been exposed to and have therefore become accustomed to during the task – or have learned in other words.

3.2.3 Feature Distribution Learning: An Example

The feature distribution learning (FDL) methodology was introduced in Chetverikov et al. (2016, see 2019 for a tutorial on FDL). Chetverikov et al. (2016) asked their observers to search for an oddly oriented line in a heterogeneously oriented set of distractor lines and respond whether the oddly oriented target was in the top three rows or bottom three rows of a six-by-six array of lines. The thirty-five distractor lines all came from a certain distribution while the target was randomly chosen from outside the range of the distractor distribution. Observers searched for a target among distractors from the same distractor distribution for four to six trials in a row (termed 'learning trials' since they were introduced for learning the statistics of the distribution). The learning was confirmed by showing that response times during the learning trials became faster and more accurate the more often the distractors from the same orientation distribution were presented on consecutive learning trials. But what information exactly do observers pick up on those learning trials?

After each sequence of learning trials in Chetverikov et al. (2016), observers' expectations were implicitly assessed on a so-called test trial (the observers were unaware that this was a test trial – to them this was just another search trial). The target and distractors were now selected randomly from the whole orientation feature space with the restriction that the distractors had to be sufficiently different (60–120 degrees apart) from the target to keep the search from becoming too difficult. This simple paradigm enabled the uncovering of internal representations of previously learned distractor distributions. Recall that the role-reversal effects are assumed to reflect violations of expectations (Chetverikov & Kristjánsson, 2015; Kristjánsson & Driver, 2008). The size of the role-reversal effect may therefore be assumed to reflect the degree to which a given feature value is expected or unexpected relative to other features (Figure 4B). If observers learned the distribution on the learning trials, we might speculate that this distribution learning would be reflected in the role-reversal effects. And the results of Chetverikov et al. (2016) were indeed the first to confirm that the variability of the previously learned distribution is reflected in the shape of the curve showing the role-reversal effects (measured in the response times). That is, distributions with a larger range had a 'wider' response time curve, and the highest point of the RT curve (depicting the largest role-reversal effects) was at the mean of the distribution. This matches findings with other approaches discussed in Section 3.1, suggesting that variability in environmental stimuli is encoded by the visual system.

However, the most important lesson from the results in Chetverikov et al. (2016) was that observers encoded variability at a surprisingly high level of detail: If the shape of the learning trial distribution was Gaussian, the shape of the curve showing the role-reversal effects (in response times) reflected this, while if its shape was uniform, this was also reflected in the shape of the curve reflecting the role-reversal effects (Figure 5A). Notably, the range (or, in another experiment, standard deviation) of the two distributions was equated.

These results demonstrated that observers could learn the shape of distractor distributions, and that the distributions are not simply represented as a mean and then perhaps with an estimate of the variance in the ensemble. Notably Chetverikov et al. (2017b, experiment 2) then demonstrated that learning of whether distributions are uniform or Gaussian could emerge after only two learning trials (in other words, two 'exemplars') from the distribution, showing that these statistics could be quickly picked up, although there was also clear evidence that the representations became more accurate with more learning trials.

As Chetverikov et al. (2019) argued, the FDL methodology and logic are in many ways similar to neurophysiological decoding measures used, for example, in fMRI and EEG studies. The responses on individual trials are used to estimate the otherwise unobservable internal representation of a complex visual stimulus. The FDL method might be considered a behavioural alternative to those, enabling an understanding of how information is represented in the brain. For example, fMRI decoding has revealed the uncertainty in visual representations – where the likelihood of a stimulus can be decoded (Chetverikov & Jehee, 2023; van Bergen et al., 2015) and similar findings on decoding have emerged in neurophysiology (Walker et al., 2020). However, FDL is limited in predicting representations on single trials because of the sparse data that is available, so the aggregate representations are analysed instead (but see Chetverikov et al., 2020 where double-target search is used to overcome this problem).

3.2.4 Learning Colour Distributions

After demonstrating how observers can learn to distinguish Gaussian and uniform orientation distributions, Chetverikov et al. (2017c) then tested the learning of colour distributions, again using the feature distribution learning method. This time the observers had to find the oddly coloured diamond among a large set of distractor diamonds (thirty-five in total) and then report whether

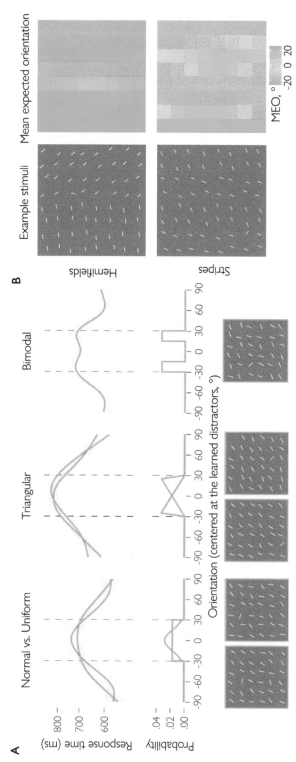

Figure 5 Feature distribution learning shows that variability in the visual world is encoded at a high level of detail. A. Observers encode different distribution shapes. Even though the stimuli generated from a uniform and a normal distribution, or two triangular distributions (bottom) might look similar, FDL studies shows that observers take into account the differences between them. The response time curve for a uniform distribution (orange) is flat within the range of the distribution (dashed lines) matching the distribution probability density function shown below. In contrast, for a normal distribution, the response times decrease monotonically, again matching the distribution shape. For the two triangular distributions, the response times curves are skewed following the corresponding probability density functions. Finally, for

Caption for Figure 5 (cont.)

a bimodal distribution, the response time curves also indicate bimodality. Plots are based on the data from Chetverikov et al. (2016, 2017b). B. When stimuli vary differently in different parts of the visual space, this is reflected in the properties of recovered representations. For example, when left and right hemifields have orientation distributions with different means, the mean expected orientation (MEO, see Figure 4 and the main text for details) track these differences. The reconstructed maps of MEO match the true distribution mean (±20°). However, there are also biases as the MEO's are shifted towards the other distribution at the boundaries between them (i.e., for central columns in the hemifields arrangement, MEO are shifted towards 0° while for other columns they match the true means precisely). This demonstrates the hierarchical nature of mental representations: rather than simply being based on the visual input at a given location, the information is integrated from multiple neighbouring patches. This figure is adapted from Figure 3 from Chetverikov & Kristjánsson (2022)

provided under CCBY-4.0 license.

the target diamond had a notch at the top, bottom, right, or left (all of the 36 stimuli had notches at one of these locations). Again, the distractors on learning trials came from different distributions (this time, colour distributions). The colours were selected from a psychophysically linearized colour space (Witzel & Gegenfurtner, 2013, 2015) to avoid unwanted influences from nonlinearities in colour space. Chetverikov et al. (2017c) found that response times during the learning trials became faster and accuracy increased as the distractors from the same colour distributions were consecutively presented. The role-reversal effects followed the distributions from the learning trials, showing how observers could learn the full distributions of colour ensembles – more specifically, whether they were uniform or Gaussian. This result was quite surprising, since subjectively, the search among the two distributions appeared to be quite similar. It was also important in demonstrating learning of distribution shape for another dimension than orientation, increasing the generalizability of the original FDL findings on orientation in Chetverikov et al. (2016).

3.2.5 Sensitivity to Different Statistical Aspects of Distributions

Learning of more complex distributions than uniform or Gaussian distributions has since been tested. Initially, Chetverikov et al. (2016, experiment 4), demonstrated that not only could observers determine whether the distractor distribution was uniform or Gaussian, but observers could even learn whether the distributions were positively or negatively skewed (triangular distributions in Figure 5A). Even more surprisingly, in Chetverikov et al. (2017b) observers were then able to learn whether oriented distractor lines presented during learning trials were drawn from a unimodal or bimodal distribution (see also Chetverikov et al., 2020). But interestingly, this learning of bimodality only emerged after a larger set of learning trials than for example learning of uniform versus Gaussian distributions (or approximately eight trials), with thirty-five exemplars from the distribution on each trial (Chetverikov et al. 2017b, experiment 2, had shown that basics of distributions could be learned within two trials). In essence, this makes sense, since with increasing complexity more information should be needed to determine the true nature of the underlying distribution. This is a very clear example of the learning and representation of high-complexity ensembles that go far beyond any representations of summary statistics.

3.2.6 Are Irrelevant Distribution Statistics Learned?

Hansmann-Roth et al. (2019) investigated how much information can be learned simultaneously about different aspects of feature distributions. The detailed learning for colour and orientation shown separately in previous experiments already involved the learning of large amounts of information – potentially quite taxing for the visual system if the goal is to pick this information up in 'parallel' for different feature distributions. Importantly, the distributions in these previous cases were always task-relevant. In the initial attempt of Hansmann-Roth et al. (2019), two feature dimensions could simultaneously vary while the participants searched for lines of differing orientations and colours, that could vary simultaneously but importantly did so independently. The aim of Hansmann-Roth et al. was to measure whether an irrelevant feature distribution influenced the learning of a task-relevant distribution. While considerable learning of feature distributions was observed, in particular for colour, the results also showed that a second irrelevant feature distribution (in this case orientation) could not be learned in detail (while some basic aspects of these distributions were learned). The results of Hansmann-Roth et al. therefore revealed notable limitations on what information can be learned, at least within similar time periods as the orientation learning, or colour learning, on their own, could occur in.

Pascucci et al. (2022) then tested the role of the task in feature distribution learning. Instead of an active search task during the learning trials, observers *passively* viewed the displays on the learning trials and role-reversal effects were then tested as in previous FDL experiments. Specifically, Pascucci et al. (2022) tested whether the learning of the visual feature distributions occurs during passive viewing of the ensembles. Note that feature distribution learning had in all previous demonstrations been found in tasks requiring active visual search for a singleton target that differed from the distractors. Also, the results of Hansmann-Roth et al. (2019) suggested that the shapes of task-irrelevant distributions are not picked up. The results of Pascucci et al. showed that passive exposure to distributions of visual features in the absence of an explicit search task led to similar role-reversal effects as previously seen (although the difference between uniform and Gaussian distribution shapes was not significant). But in an important manipulation they found that passive viewing of displays containing no target (in other words, no orientation singleton) did not lead to distribution learning. So while active search was not required, the presence of a singleton was necessary. Pascucci et al. speculated that the irrelevant singleton triggered attentional capture on passive trials. This may have led to the automatic segmentation of the oddly oriented item from the rest of the stimuli, which may have created at least a coarse representation of the shape of the underlying distribution. But importantly, they found that this did not occur without the singleton. Pascucci et al. (2022) speculated that the automatic singleton detection created a relatively coarse representation of the statistical distribution that the rest of the items came from. Active search for the singleton as in other FDL experiments enables, on the other hand, a more precise representation of the distractor distribution to emerge.

It is interesting to compare these findings with what has been observed in the literature on summary statistics. There is indeed evidence in the summary statistics literature that task-irrelevant statistics can be learned (Oriet & Brand, 2013). Chong & Treisman (2003) argued that 'statistical descriptors' are computed automatically when attention is distributed over a display, which could mean that they are picked up 'for free', or do not require explicit encoding, nor claim resources. Also, when irrelevant variation in stimuli is predictable, this can aid visual search (Corbett & Melcher, 2014). Oriet & Hozempa (2016) tested observers' ability to reproduce global statistical char-acteristics of a set, after they attended to properties irrelevant to this judgment. While observers were able to produce mean and endpoints of a distribution there was little or no evidence of any learning of distribution shape. So the summary statistics literature seems to indicate that some learning of irrelevant ensembles can occur, although there also seems to be evidence that there are notable limits on this (see also Hansmann-Roth et al., 2021, and further discussion in Sections 3.2.11 and 3.3).

3.2.7 Do Observers Integrate Information about Different Feature Distributions and Their Spatial Locations?

At this point, we can ask whether the feature distribution learning method enables insight into how more complex visual representations that covary on more than one feature, or are tied to certain spatial locations, can be built. Can information about different distributions be combined, which would seem like a necessary step for this information to be used for the building of representations of real-world scenes and objects? This question was addressed in Chetverikov & Kristjánsson (2022), and their results involved a key demonstration. They won-dered whether the representations that are uncovered in FDL studies can provide the basis for 'normal' vision within more complex multidimensional environ-ments. The aim was to understand whether the visual system has access to information about not only *how* the features are distributed, but also where they are and what other features they may be combined with. Note that this is a different question from the one asked by Hansmann-Roth et al. (2019, described in Section 3.2.6) who investigated simultaneous learning of two unrelated distri-butions (one of them being task-irrelevant) but the question that Chetverikov & Kristjánsson (2022) investigated revolves around their *integration*.

Chetverikov and Kristjánsson (2022) randomly split the distractor set on each trial in two parts that differed in their orientation distributions. These two parts were then assigned different colours or placed in separate locations. Chetverikov and Kristjánsson then tested whether observers associate a given colour (location) with a given orientation distribution by using test targets of different colours or in different locations. But, unsurprisingly perhaps, the representations were noisier (i.e., had higher standard deviations) when orientation was paired with colour compared to the condition where the two orientation distributions had different spatial locations. When the display was split into four columns by orientation, instead of split by half, there was still integration of spatial information with the orientation distribution, but again, it was more noisy. Furthermore, in both cases there was noticeable skew in the recovered probabilistic representations, indicating that representations of orientation distributions of different colours or placed in different locations had a mutual influence on the response time curves.

Chetverikov and Kristjánsson (2022) also showed that the representations are hierarchical in nature. This was evident from the bias in recovered representations towards the other distribution of colour or location that can be seen in a 'map' of recovered mean expected orientation for the case of location-orientation combination (Figure 5B). When the left and the right visual field have different orientations, the bias occurs on the boundary between them, suggesting that observers account for local as well as global differences in distribution parameters. This means that the variability of visual stimuli is represented at different levels.

The variation on the FDL method that Chetverikov & Kristjánsson (2022) used, essentially involved assessing the interactions of different distributions (location and orientation on the one hand and orientation and colour on the other). Chetverikov & Kristjánsson (2022) found that observers can not only encode feature distributions in scenes containing two different distributions but more importantly, also combine them. The results revealed that observers' representations tended to reflect the physical distribution of the stimuli for a given location or a given colour. This showed that not only can distribution representations for different features (colour and orientation) be bound together but they can be bound with locations as well.

The key insight was therefore that variability in distributions can be represented, but most importantly, that the variability can be integrated with spatial locations and other features (colour) that are *differently* distributed across the visual field. Chetverikov & Kristjánsson (2022) argued that these results were the strongest evidence available for the idea that the brain builds probabilistic representations of incoming visual stimuli (see Section 4.2). The important bottom line from this work was that it demonstrated how probabilistic representations can be generated and integrated across feature dimensions, and can then

serve as building blocks for higher-level visual processes such as object construc-
tion and scene processing. Again, this result argues strongly against accounts of
visual representations that assume that they are based on summary statistics.

3.2.8 Are Representations of Environmental Statistics Accurate at Individual Time Points?

Like most other approaches that involve implicit assessment of the key vari-
ables, feature distribution learning studies rely on the aggregation of data from
many trials to infer the properties of mental representations. This places limits
on what can be inferred about the representation of variability at a given
moment in time. It is always possible that what appears, for example, as
a bimodal representation when the data is aggregated, is a combination of
unimodal representations with different mean values on different trials.

To address this issue, and to assess whether the feature representations FDL
studies have revealed are accurate at individual time points, Chetverikov et al.
(2020) used a dual-target paradigm where observers had to find two targets on each
trial. This manipulation was important as it allows the sampling of *two* points of the
represented distribution at an individual time point (instead of the aggregation over
time in the previous FDL studies that are described above). This can provide a more
accurate estimate of the shape of what is represented *at a given moment*.
Chetverikov et al. (2020) tested the learning of a bimodal distribution and, as in
Chetverikov et al. (2017b), targets on *test* trials which could correspond to various
regions of orientation space that distractors on preceding trials were drawn from,
and could, for example, have feature values that fall in between the modes of the
bimodal orientation distribution, or that fall outside the range of the previous
distribution.

Observers were told that they should respond to each of the two targets as
soon as they found them. Importantly, they were told not to wait until both
targets were found but to report by keypress in which quadrant of the search
display the target was as soon as they found it and only then find the next one.
Similar logic of learning trials followed by test trials as used in other FDL
studies was used for this paradigm, where role-reversal effects between target
and distractor distributions were measured.

Under a strong version of a probabilistic account of visual representations,
the templates would include information about both peaks of a bimodal distribution as well as the trough between them (see, e.g., Tanrıkulu et al., 2021a). In
other words, the assumption is that observers would develop an accurate
internal model for the task and the template would accurately reflect the
information about the full probability distribution. Alternatively, the templates

might include only a single peak (e.g., the attended one), or might reflect only the summary statistics denoting the midpoint between the two distributions. For the two-target search task, Chetverikov et al. (2020) reasoned that if observers accurately encode a bimodal distribution, on test trials with a target on a peak and a target between peaks of the learning distribution, targets between the peaks (associated with a lower distractor probability) should be reported before targets on peaks, reflecting that they are easier to find. If only one peak is encoded or if the whole distribution is averaged, targets on peaks would be associated with a lower distractor probability and should be reported no later (showing no increase in role-reversal effects) than targets between the peaks (associated with lower distractor probability in this case).

The results clearly indicated that observers' representation of the learning distribution was bimodal – and importantly bimodal at individual moments in time. Observers were slower to find targets on the peaks of the bimodal learning distribution while targets outside the learning distribution were found the fastest. The slowest response times occurred when the two targets came from the two peaks of the bimodal distribution. And when the two targets were from between the peaks and from outside the distribution, the outside targets tended to be found before the between-peak target. This was clear evidence that the bimodality of the distribution was represented, that both of its peaks were *simultaneously* represented, and the smaller probability of a distractor coming from the trough between the two peaks was represented, as well. This showed that the representation was this detailed at this particular moment in time and that the representations did not simply reflect performance aggregated over time. The distribution – in the moment – represented the actual probability values.

Chetverikov et al. (2020) also simulated predictions for the search performance of the models assuming bimodal, single-template, and averaged representations. The simulation where bimodal representations were assumed, was by far the best at predicting the observed performance both in terms of response times and the order in which the targets were reported. Importantly by using double-target search Chetverikov et al. were able to demonstrate that the results of previous experiments where observers learned the distribution on average, cannot be explained by a combination of different decision rules applied on different test trials, but that the representation is bimodal at a given moment in time.

3.2.9 Does Feature Distribution Learning Impact Search Performance Only, or Perception More Generally?

The learning effects demonstrated with the feature distribution learning method would have limited importance for understanding perception in a more general sense, if the only benefit of the learning was to find targets in visual search tasks. It is therefore important to test whether the feature distribution learning influences perception in a more general sense.

This question has been addressed with the use of a well-documented temporal bias in perception called serial dependence (Fischer & Whitney, 2014; see Pascucci et al., 2023 for review). Rafiei et al. (2021a, 2021b) tested the effects of feature distribution learning upon serial dependence biases in the perception of orientation. Their results show how probabilistic information about feature distributions of distractors from previous trials affects orientation estimates. Rafiei et al. (2021a) tested judgments of the orientation of single oriented lines following FDL-like learning trials where their observers searched for an oddly oriented line among distractors on a number of adjacent trials – a fairly standard FDL task – and were then occasionally asked to report the orientation of the last visual search target. Rafiei et al. found that there were two opposite biases from the search stimuli that nevertheless operated simultaneously: there was an attractive bias from the recent targets of the search (similar to attractive biases in serial dependence studies, Fischer & Whitney, 2014; Pascucci et al., 2023) while the distractors caused a repulsive bias. This was an important demonstration as it showed how perception *per se* is biased by the learning processes that the FDL methods uncover (rather than simply search performance). Consistently, Chapman et al. (2023) have recently demonstrated how the similarity of targets and distractors can rapidly affect attentional tuning (see also Geng et al., 2017; Witkowski & Geng, 2019).

It is very important in this context to note that Rafiei et al. (2021b) then demonstrated that these biases did not solely apply to visual search items, but also to oriented lines that appeared *after* the search was performed and therefore played no role in the search task, showing how these biases from preceding variability influence perception in a general sense, not simply the search tasks. But while these results of Rafiei et al. are promising, there is a lot of work to be done in uncovering how the learning of the environmental statistics that FDL studies reveal operate in perception in a more general sense.

3.2.10 Picking up Variability in the Goal of the Search (the Targets) Instead of Distractors

The research that has been presented up until now, where the FDL method has been used, has clearly shown how the variability in to-be-ignored items during a selective attentional task (the distractors) is picked up and influences perception. But what about the focus of attention in these visual search tasks, or the target itself, in other words? Can observers pick up the statistics about the distributions that the target is drawn from?

Note that this is a more difficult concept to test as it is hard to expose observers to enough exemplars of targets from a distribution on single-target trials. Hansmann-Roth et al. (2022) asked this question in a task where observers had to locate the odd-one-out coloured diamond among two distractor diamonds and judge whether the target diamond had a notch at the top, bottom, left, or right (a task introduced by Bravo & Nakayama, 1992). The target on trials within the same block was either drawn from a Gaussian distribution or a uniform one. Once observers had been exposed to a large number of search trials, response times for the target revealed the shape of the underlying target distributions, just as has been seen before in previous FDL studies, but this learning required many more search trials to reliably emerge, presumably since only one exemplar appeared on each trial instead of the ensembles appearing in other FDL studies. These results of Hansmann-Roth et al. (2022) reveal a remarkable ability to assemble statistical information over time, in the form of feature distributions even when at a given moment, very little information is available about the distribution.

3.2.11 Limitations of the Feature Distribution Learning Method

Despite its advantages, the FDL method also has drawbacks. The use of visual search as the task for learning and testing representations of variability necessarily implies that observers learn information about both target distributions (Hansmann-Roth et al., 2022) and distractor distributions (e.g., Chetverikov et al., 2016). While this does not preclude comparisons between different distribution types, precise quantitative modelling of observers' behaviour requires assumptions about target or distractor representations and non-decisional components of response times (see Chetverikov & Kristjánsson, 2022 for a computational model). In other words, only a monotonic relationship between the internal representation of a distractor probability distribution and response times can be assessed without further assumptions. When a certain feature value (e.g., orientation at 45 degrees) matches distractors better, a target that has this value will lead to slower search. But it is impossible to say what is the expected probability of distractors at this value without additional assumptions. This makes quantitative estimates of distractor variability relative. That is, the FDL method can be used to determine if one condition results in a representation with more variability than another, but can only be used to determine exactly how large the represented variability is, if further assumptions are made.

The FDL method also requires relatively good search performance. Certain populations, such as small children, for example, might have difficulties with the task that are unrelated to the way they represent variability. For example, van de Cruys et al. (2021) had to simplify the task when they used FDL to study how probability distributions are learned and encoded by children. And even in this simplified version of the task, response times were considerably higher than in the previous studies using adult participants. This poses challenges for future research with such populations as longer search times might imply that the processing of stimuli is serial and therefore relies less on previous knowledge, making inferences about internal representations more difficult, among other things because of decisional influences. The FDL method could also have potential applications to research into the neural representations of visual information. This could, for example, be important in studies of patient populations. It could, as an example, be of large interest to study the performance of individuals with hemispatial neglect or blindsight on FDL-type tasks. But more efficient ways of assessing FDL would probably be needed for such applications.

Furthermore, despite revealing rapid learning in terms of the duration of individual learning blocks, the total number of trials needed to show differentiation of similar distribution shapes (uniform vs. Gaussian) is still considerable (usually 1000 trials, or more are required). Of course, other distribution parameters, such as means or variance, can be estimated more quickly.

3.2.12 Summary of the FDL Method

Overall, we are beginning to understand how the visual system uses the statistical information in recent visual input to guide behaviour. The feature distribution learning method has enabled us to uncover representations of heterogeneous stimuli in surprising detail, and has yielded results that differ markedly from traditional explicit methods (as shown by Hansmann-Roth et al., 2021 and discussed in Section 3.3). Most importantly, FDL studies show that observers can learn the shape of orientation and colour distributions within arrays containing multiple stimuli with various feature values (Chetverikov et al., 2017c). Observers integrate information over several trials to build probabilistic representations of feature distributions with complex shapes: Gaussian or uniform, skewed to the left or right, and even bimodal distributions (Chetverikov et al., 2017b, 2020). Since this method was introduced, a lot of findings have emerged that support this general notion (Chetverikov et al., 2020; Chetverikov & Kristjánsson, 2022; Hansmann-Roth et al., 2021, 2022; Pascucci et al., 2022; Rafiei et al., 2021a, 2021b; Tanrıkulu et al., 2020, 2021b). Importantly, in a key demonstration, Chetverikov and Kristjánsson (2022, see discussion in Section 3.2.7) showed that the uncovered representations can serve as building blocks for higher-level vision as revealed by their integration with the spatial distributions of stimuli and distributions of other features. Rafiei et al. (2021a, b) then showed how these representations can affect perceptual decisions directly.

The findings from FDL methods are not only interesting in how they demonstrate what can be picked up regarding the detail in the environment. They also have notable implications with regard to the broader picture of how visual perception operates that will be discussed in the following sections.

3.2.13 Other Implicit Tests of Representations of Visual Variability

While FDL is currently the most developed implicit approach for uncovering how visual variability is represented, it is certainly not the only approach. First, it is possible to infer how variability in the stimuli is represented by looking at performance in a forced-choice member identification task as a function of the feature distributions that the stimuli belong to. The basic idea is similar to the FDL method but there are some notable differences. Observers are shown a set of stimuli and asked to remember them, while later, two items are presented and the observers are required to report which one of the two was present. Thus, unlike in FDL, the observers here are explicitly instructed to remember the stimulus set even though they are not explicitly tested on their knowledge of the properties of the set. The idea is that these properties are nevertheless encoded and will affect whether items are identified as members of the memory set. For example, if observers represent stimuli by keeping track of their mean and range, then they should identify items within that range as having been presented even if they were actually not presented (a false alarm, in a sense). Such results have been found in several papers (Khayat & Hochstein, 2018, 2019; Sama et al., 2021). For example, in Khayat & Hochstein (2018), twelve circles were serially presented, each for 100 ms followed by a membership test. What participants did not know was that on some membership tests, one of the stimuli equalled the mean of the set, and or a non-member of the set, outside the distribution range. Participants tended to choose circles close to the mean while tending to reject stimuli outside of the range.

However, it is not clear whether it is the range specifically, some other measure of variability (e.g., variance), or the full probability distribution that observers represented in these studies. In partial support of the latter possibility, Sama and colleagues (2021) also found that when a skewed distribution was used instead of the previously tested symmetrical distributions, observers were less likely to identify the members of a long tail of the distribution as previously seen. This is in line with the earlier evidence for representations of distribution shape from FDL studies (Chetverikov et al., 2016, 2017c).

Acerbi and colleagues (2012) used a very different approach to determine what observers can learn about the variability in a stimulus set in a duration estimation task. Observers were shown visual flashes where their duration was randomly sampled from a given probability distribution (e.g., uniform, peaked, and bimodal duration distributions). Their task was to reproduce the duration of the flashes by pressing and holding a mouse button for a time period equal to the flash duration. In the training part, which continued until the observers' performance had plateaued (500–1500 trials per observer in each condition in each experiment), the observers implicitly learned the parameters of the variability of the stimuli. The responses in the test part (1000 trials) were then used to recover how this variability is represented. This is possible because the computational model of the duration estimation would predict different response patterns depending on the nature of the internal representations of variability in the stimuli. Acerbi et al. found that the recovered representations ('priors') were consistent with the actual distributions of stimulus features up to the third statistical moment (mean, variance, skewness). However, in contrast with FDL results, there was no evidence that observers could learn further aspects of the distribution shape, as bimodal distributions did not lead to bimodal representations.

3.3 Implicit versus Explicit Encoding of Variability

Having discussed different methodologies testing the nature of variability representations, it is important to consider whether implicit and explicit tests of how observers represent variability test the same aspect of how variability is represented. It is quite possible that explicit tasks prompt observers to use some specific easy-to-access heuristics, like remembering the items most different from the rest, while implicit tasks rely more on the overall impression of the set of stimuli and therefore include more information about the true nature of the underlying distribution. The task requirements for the two may differ, requiring different information. And this also raises the question of whether different neural mechanisms may be responsible for performing the two tasks. On the other hand, it is also possible that regardless of the type of task, the same information is used. To answer this question, we will consider whether implicit and explicit tests have access to the same amount of information and whether they can both be used for more complex features as well as for more complex statistics of the stimulus probability distributions.

3.3.1 Amount of Information Required

Morgan et al. (2008) varied the amount of external noise in an orientation variance discrimination task to determine how participants perform compared to an ideal observer. In particular, they modelled the performance (measured in just noticeable differences, *JNDs*) of an observer that they assumed would use a certain number of randomly selected items out of the whole set of 121 Gabor elements for representing the whole sample. They estimated that participants performed similarly to an ideal observer that sampled only three to ten elements. This does not mean that observers actually sample some of the stimuli: this is just a way to quantify how much information is used. They might use other strategies than random sampling or use different estimates of distributions (e.g., range instead of variance). Similar estimates of effective sample size 6–8 were obtained by Solomon (2010) with a stimulus set of eight Gabor patches. Whitney and Yamanashi Leib (2018) have then proposed the $\sqrt{N}$ law where observers behave as if $\sqrt{N}$ stimuli from the ensemble are sampled (where N is the number of stimuli in an ensemble). While these accounts certainly do not necessarily mean that observers engage in sampling, their behaviour is nevertheless consistent with the sampling of just a few elements, perhaps weighted by their salience as Kanaya et al. (2018) observed (see also Iakovlev & Utochkin, 2021). In other words, observers perform well in explicit tests even with just a few items present and their performance improves very slowly when the number of items is increased (see Corbett et al., 2023, for a recent discussion of sampling in ensemble perception). This suggests that a large amount of information is lost in explicit variance discrimination tasks.

How much information is used in the case of implicit tests? While we do not have decisive answers to this question yet, the number would seem to have to be high to catch the shape of the distributions. To address this, Chetverikov et al. (2017d) tested learning of distributions of oriented lines varying the set size of the ensembles on learning trials. Chetverikov et al. (2017d) found that large set sizes (thirty-six lines in an orientation singleton task) were necessary for robust feature distribution learning. When the set size was 24, learning was far less strong, and distribution shape was not learned, and the learning was even less evident with set sizes of 14 and 8. Note that the sparseness of the displays for the lower set sizes was not the reason for this, as with dense displays where set-size was varied but interitem distance was equated, a similar effect of set size was observed. The set size findings seem to indicate that observers pick up the distribution properties by aggregating information over the whole display and, unlike explicit judgments, this learning requires large amounts of sensory data. This is supported by the fact that the learning improves gradually with increased numbers of learning trials (the representations are, for example, most accurate following up to eleven learning trials for a bimodal distribution; Chetverikov et al., 2017b). Again, this shows that the FDL findings are inconsistent with the proposed subsampling strategy. It is therefore likely to be fundamentally different from what is measured with explicit tests in the literature on summary statistics that seems consistent with subsampling or generally, that the available information is underutilized.

Most studies of variability perception have focused on low-level features, such as colour, orientation, or brightness. For more complex features, the ability to assess the mean is well established (see Corbett et al., 2023; Whitney & Yamanashi Leib, 2018 for reviews) but there is only limited evidence that the variability of more complex features can be represented as well. In particular, Haberman and colleagues (2015b) tested whether observers can estimate heterogeneity in facial expressions by using adjustment and forced-choice discrimination tasks. They found that performance was much better than chance level indicating that variability in facial expressions is encoded by observers. Importantly, the errors were smaller with upright faces compared to faces shown upside down. This suggests that it was indeed the variability in facial expression that was encoded and not some other lower-level feature. Mijalli et al. (2023; see also Daniels et al., 2017) also found that judgements of ethnoracial diversity reflect the diversity in the presented stimuli and furthermore that these judgements depend on the gender diversity in stimuli. Such 'spillover' effects were also observed by Mijalli and colleagues for combinations of high-level (ethnoracial) and low-level (colour) variation: when faces are presented on a background of coloured circles, ethnoracial diversity is rated higher when circles are more variable (see also the discussion of adaptation effects in Section 3.3.1). This suggests that there might be common mechanisms behind high-level and low-level variability estimates, but further studies are necessary to see if these effects can be replicated when controlling for demand characteristics and other potential confounds.

Hansmann-Roth et al. (2023) tested feature distribution learning of distributions based on stimulus shape, in particular a linearized circular shape space developed by Li et al. (2020). Hansmann-Roth et al. found that learning of the shape of distributions (either a uniform or a Gaussian distribution) did not occur for this shape space. However, observers were able to learn the mean and variance of the distributions as in the cases of explicit estimation or discrimination of such summary statistics found in other studies (Corbett et al., 2023; Whitney & Yamanashi Leib, 2018). This may indicate that precise feature distribution learning is limited to relatively simple features, since the processing of shape may require more sophisticated neural mechanisms than for processing colour or orientation. The object recognition literature indicates that shapes are assembled from different parts, parts that differ in salience which may involve relatively complicated integration of basic properties (Biederman, 1987; Hoffman & Richards, 1984; Marr et al., 1978). This is also broadly consistent with the lack of simultaneous learning of colour and shape observed by Hansmann-Roth et al. (2019).

3.3.3 Access to Information about More Complex Distribution Parameters

Is it possible that both explicit and implicit tests can be used to access more complex parameters of feature distributions? As we highlighted in Section 3.2, in implicit studies using the FDL method, the observers are sensitive to different distribution parameters, such as mean and variance, but more importantly also skew and the overall shape of the feature distributions (Chetverikov et al., 2016, 2017b, 2020). On the explicit side, studies of the perception of ensembles have over the years tended to focus on simple summary statistics – in particular on questions such as what the mean or the variance of a particular ensemble is. The studies have typically involved displaying an ensemble and explicitly asking for judgments about the mean or variance of the ensemble – yielding findings showing that observers can indeed make such estimates. Notably, there is no evidence that observers can estimate the shape of distributions in forced-choice tasks (e.g., skew, kurtosis, or whether they have more than one mode). When such questions have been explicitly addressed with the methods typically used in the ensemble literature, no sensitivity to higher-order statistics (higher than the second moment, e.g., skewness or kurtosis) has been found (Atchley & Andersen, 1995; Dakin, 2001; Dakin & Watt, 1997; Hansmann-Roth et al., 2021; Tran et al., 2017). The explicit reproduction tasks seem to be an exception where observers seem to be able to reproduce some higher-order aspects of distribution (e.g., skew or bimodality) in extreme cases. Importantly, feature distribution learning methods have on the other hand revealed that observers can learn far more detail of variability within visual environments than the studies using explicit tasks indicate.

Note that this difference in sensitivity to more complex distribution parameters between implicit and explicit methods cannot be attributed to differences in the amount of information available to participants. Hansmann-Roth et al. (2021; see Section 3.3.4 for a more detailed discussion) implemented the explicit and implicit tests within the same overall design following previous FDL studies (multiple learning trials followed by a test). However, no evidence of sensitivity to distribution shape was found for explicit judgments. In contrast, Chetverikov et al. (2017b) found that already one to two learning trials are enough to learn simpler distribution shapes, although more other (bimodal) distributions might take more time. Both studies argue against the idea that the amount of information in the stimuli is a crucial factor when contrasting implicit and explicit tasks (as opposed to the amount of information used by participants, Section 3.3.1).

3.3.4 Do Summary Statistics Judgments and Feature Distribution Learning Share Common Mechanisms?

Are there common mechanisms responsible for performance on explicit and implicit tests of variability perception? In other words, are the two mechanisms related at all? An important result was reported by Hansmann-Roth et al. (2021) where this was tested directly. Explicit reports of the mean, variance and shape of distributions were compared against the implicit FDL measures. As explained in Section 3.2, the FDL measures are implicit since they rely on role-reversal effects and in essence observers do not have any idea of whether they are being probed with regard to mean, variance or shape. Hansmann-Roth et al. contrasted explicit (probing with forced-choice discrimination) and implicit methods (role reversals on test trials, as in FDL methods) in a colour search task similar to the one used by Chetverikov et al. (2017c). Hansmann-Roth et al. found that observers could readily distinguish distractor sets from previous learning trials with different mean and variance using the explicit discrimination method, but importantly, they cannot do this for distribution shape. In this regard, Hansmann-Roth et al. (2021) replicated earlier findings using explicit tests discussed in the previous section but now in the conditions typical for FDL studies where observers have information from multiple learning trials with large number of stimuli preceding the test. For the implicit FDL method, on the other hand, there was strong evidence for learning of all three aspects (mean, variance, and shape of the underlying distributions) in the response time curves.

Importantly, Hansmann-Roth et al. (2021) also assessed the relationship between performance on different tasks. They used an ideal observer model to infer the amount of noise (inverse of the slope of the psychometric curve) affecting the internal representation of mean and variance and the variance of the internal representation (the width of the response time curve) in the implicit task. Importantly, all three estimates depended on the internal noise in the visual system. Hansmann-Roth et al. (2021) reasoned that if the explicit and implicit tasks have common mechanisms then there should be shared sources of noise and the estimates of noise in the explicit tasks and variance in the implicit task should be correlated. Indeed, they found a strong correlation across observers for the noise estimates in explicit mean and variance estimation tasks. However, the variance estimate of the implicit FDL task was not correlated with the other two. This was a crucial result since it suggested that the overlap in noise sources is at best, very small, arguing that different mechanisms are involved in explicit and implicit assessments of the characteristics of stimulus ensembles. While this lack of correlation by itself is not enough to make any strong conclusions, in combination with a notable lack of results showing the ability to discriminate complex properties (Section 3.3.3) and the differences related to the amount of information utilized in explicit and implicit tests (Section 3.3.1), this suggests a dissociation of mechanisms of implicit and explicit tests.

3.3.5 What Limits Explicit Assessment of Variability?

The literature on ensemble perception has suggested that far less information is represented than is available in the environment. While this is likely to be true in a general sense, many findings in the ensemble perception and summary statistic literature are at odds with the findings that studies using the FDL method have revealed. Far more information about the statistics of the environment seems to be available for performance than summary statistics studies seem to indicate. It is notable that summary statistics studies typically rely on explicit reports to assess distributions, including shape. But we think it is important to highlight that such estimation is not a task that the visual system typically has to perform. The primary purpose of vision is not to count statistical properties, or to explicitly estimate statistical properties, but instead the goal is successful *interaction* with the world, a point emphasized strongly in James Gibson's ecological approach to perception (Gibson, 1950, 1962) recently re-emphasized by Kristjánsson & Draschkow (2021). In this light, it makes sense that even though the information about distribution shape is not available for explicit reporting, it is available for interactions with the world.

The results of Hansmann-Roth et al. (2021) and other studies discussed in Sections 3.1 and 3.3.3 suggest that when observers are explicitly asked about representations, they cannot report the detail that they can nevertheless act on (using it to speed their search in the case of FDL). Their performance at reporting distribution shape seems to reflect that when the information has to be explicitly reported, it is not available for that. On the other hand, when the information is to be used for successful interactions with the world, it is clearly available. What this means is that detailed representations are implicit and cannot easily be accessed with explicit reports. The explicit reproduction tasks may force observers into lower-dimensional spaces of possibilities than those that we use for interactions with the world. This could reflect that the discrimination task is not a natural one for the visual system while the search in FDL tasks better resembles what natural vision is used for. Hansmann-Roth et al. speculated that this dissociation was potentially related to widely known different pathways for perception and action (Goodale & Milner, 1992; Mishkin & Ungerleider, 1982), in the extrastriate ventral and dorsal visual streams, respectively.

Note however that there is evidence from studies of the averaging of ensembles of orientated triangles, that ensemble averaging is influenced by skew. Iakovlev and Utochkin (2023) found that the estimates of averages were systematically skewed towards the mode (away from the mean) a bias that increased as the distance between the mean and the mode became larger. Similarly, Kim and Chong (2020) found that congruency in skew or variance between the presented and the test stimuli makes mean estimation more precise. They asked observers to explicitly reproduce the mean of a set of circles, but notably, observers reproduced the means on another set of circles (rather than the more typical single test item for estimation). They varied the set size, variance, and skewness between the example set and probe set. They found that keeping these properties constant improved performance on the mean estimation task. The shape of the distribution therefore influenced the explicit judgement, but it seemingly did so implicitly, because the distribution shape was not to be reported (which could have been a useful comparison). The results of Im et al. (2020) where observers explicitly judged category boundaries (whether circular objects belonged to the 'large' set or the 'small' one) show how distribution statistics, including distribution shape, play a role in the judgments (it is not discounted, or ignored in the estimates). These findings indicate that encoding of distribution parameters also occurs with the designs typically used in studies with explicit tests, but it is difficult for observers to access these parameters in an explicit way, consistent with what Hansmann-Roth et al. (2021) observed.

It seems somewhat paradoxical that skew, for example, influences explicit mean estimates but not explicit skew estimates, or that the shape of the feature distribution is reflected in response times in FDL studies but not in observers' performance in a 2AFC task testing shape discrimination. Why do the explicit tests not reveal the knowledge about distributions that is available? As argued in the opening paragraph of this section, the artificial nature of forced-choice discrimination tests may be the reason, although mean and variance discrimination are perhaps no less artificial than skew discrimination. Alternatively, particular strategies that observers use in explicit tasks might preclude the use of knowledge about more complex distribution parameters. For example, using range is a viable heuristic for variance discrimination but is useless for skew discrimination. Anecdotally, experimenters using the FDL paradigm have found that they can discriminate uniform and Gaussian stimuli by focusing on the uniformity of the distribution (i.e., the lack of a pronounced mode) as a cue. But this is because they are aware that there are two specific distributions and know how they differ from each other. Observers who do not have this knowledge might invent other less useful heuristics during their performance.

Interestingly, in explicit reproduction tasks observers can point out some properties of the feature distribution, such as skew or bimodality (Oriet & Hozempa, 2016; Tran et al., 2017). However, this happens only in the case of extreme examples and also with high degree of imprecision. We believe that this also demonstrates the limits of explicit judgments, because it stands to reason that if, for example, there are just two orientations shown over and over, observers will learn that the distribution is 'bimodal'. The fact that such extreme examples are needed to demonstrate the ability to explicitly reproduce the distribution suggests that observers engage with the distribution in a different way than in the case of implicit tests.

In this context, it is interesting to read more than twenty-year old arguments from the change blindness literature where similar points are made (with reference to 'grand illusion' arguments of the paucity of visual representations, Cohen et al., 2016; O'Regan, 1992). Thornton & Fernandez-Duque (2000, p. 25) argued, 'Studies of change blindness are considered to be important evidence in support of perception as a "Grand Illusion." However, these studies of change blindness, as with earlier studies that invoke the Grand Illusion, typically require observers to make explicit reports. Thus, while they may provide direct evidence about perceptual awareness, such findings are less informative about perceptual representation'.

We believe that the findings that we have reviewed here make it obvious that the learning is implicit and is therefore presumably mediated by mechanisms that do not make a direct contribution to consciousness. It may be informative to look at other phenomena of how non-conscious processing influences visual performance. Examples can be found in neuropsychology, in phenomena like blindsight, where people can perform various visuomotor tasks despite damage to the primary visual cortex (Danckert & Goodale, 2000). Another example is priming effects from stimuli that are missed in neglect (Kristjánsson et al., 2005; Saevarsson et al., 2008). Studies of such patient populations along with neuro-imaging or electrophysiology might provide information about neural loci of FDL and about which regions are necessary for such learning to emerge.

In sum, explicit and implicit tests of variability seem to reflect different aspects of visual perception. During explicit tests, observers seem to be able to utilize less information about the stimuli and do not have access to the same level of complexity about the parameters of feature distributions and may rely more on heuristics and therefore miss details in their task performance.

3.4 Current Progress in the Understanding of Representations of Variability

So, how is variability in the visual input represented? We have highlighted the results obtained with different methodologies from forced-choice tests to implicit feature distribution learning. Overall, it seems that the method used for testing variability representations strongly influences the estimates of what is represented. More implicit methods show a higher degree of detail in representations, including the representation of the shape of the feature distribution, while more explicit methods seem limited to their variance or range. As we have argued in a previous section, this might reflect reliance on *heuristics* in explicit judgements. Knowledge of the finer details of variability representations has now been confirmed in many studies with different methods suggesting that future studies using explicit tests should be interpreted with an emphasis on what observers do in these tests rather than what they represent (see also Kay et al., 2023).

We have not touched upon the issue of neural representation of variability. This is partly because there have not been many studies on this issue, which can, in turn, be explained by the fact that we can expect that the variability in the stimuli will be naturally represented in neural responses. This is illustrated by a recent population coding model by Utochkin et al. (2023) that shows how read-out from a population of neurons pooling over multiple stimuli in a set can be used for various tasks that we have discussed (e.g., 2AFC variability discrimination or feature distribution learning). In other words, the representation of variability is present in the neural population responses and can be either read out in an explicit fashion or used implicitly in neural computations (see also Walker et al., 2023). For example, changes in motion coherence (variability in the direction of moving dots) correspond to differential responses of neural populations in classic visual areas, similarly to internal fluctuations in sensory uncertainty (e.g., Braddick et al., 2001; Chetverikov & Jehee, 2023; Hebart et al., 2012; McKeefry et al., 1997; Rees et al., 2000). On the other hand, Witkowski & Geng (2023) recently studied how a target varying across trials in a visual search task is encoded in the brain with fMRI and suggested that the mean and variability of target features could be encoded independently. They were able to decode the mean target colour using the multivariate pattern analysis (a linear classifier) in prefrontal cortex (dorsolateral prefrontal cortex and inferior frontal junction) as well as occipital cortex (V1–V3) while variability was reflected in the overall BOLD signal strength in the same regions of prefrontal cortex. However, the overall BOLD strength might reflect other factors confounded with variability (attentional engagement, task difficulty) making the unequivocal interpretation of the findings difficult.

Interestingly, information about variability accumulated at different time-scales might be represented in the brain in different ways. Vilares et al. (2012) used a variant of a centroid estimation task where participants had to guess the location of a hidden target based on several points spread around it. They varied both the variability of the points on individual trials ('likelihood') and the variability of the hidden locations across trials ('prior'). They found that while the changes in 'likelihood' were correlated with changes in the fMRI BOLD signal in the visual cortex, changes in the 'prior' were correlated with activity in other regions (putamen, amygdala, orbitofrontal cortex, and the insula). However, such evidence can be difficult to interpret because of add-itional factors that may affect performance, such as task difficulty and attention fluctuations, that could explain the correlations. Future studies using approaches that reconstruct probabilistic representation in the cortex in a more direct fashion (e.g., van Bergen & Jehee, 2021; Walker et al., 2023) might shed more light on the question of neural representation of variability.

4 Discussion

4.1 Rich or Sparse Experience, Overflow and the Grand Illusion

Understanding the perception of variability is important as this can aid the resolution of a long-standing debate, sometimes called the question of overflow (e.g., Block, 2011). The overflow view is that perceptual consciousness is richer than the information that can be cognitively accessed reflects. In contrast, others have argued that observers can only represent the very limited amount of information that observers can report and consciously attend to (Noe, 2002; O'Regan, 1992; O'Regan & Noë, 2001). This is, in essence, the claim that the detail that we think we perceive in the environment is actually a 'grand illusion' (O'Regan, 1992). More recently, Cohen et al. (2016) proposed a related pos-ition, that can be considered an attempt at a compromise, suggesting that observers only represent coarse statistical summaries outside of the focus of attention. However, this approach seems to underestimate the level of detail that the visual system can represent, as we have argued in Section 3.3 and then elaborate on in this section.

4.1.1 Evidence for the 'Grand Illusion' and Overflow Views

There is therefore something of a paradox here. On the one hand, there are powerful demonstrations of inattentional blindness where we can miss large changes to visual scenes or miss highly pertinent information in our visual field, a gorilla can walk unnoticed across a screen that we are watching if we are engaged in another task (Mack & Rock, 1998; Simons & Chabris, 1999). Change blindness studies then show how we can be surprisingly inept at noticing large changes, such as an engine missing from a jet, in visual scenes following interruptions such as from masks (Rensink et al., 1997) or from mudsplashes (O'Regan et al., 1999). Additionally, there is the literature that has sometimes been thought to reveal the paucity of our visual representations – in particular, the literature on ensemble representations that seems to indicate that we can only represent summaries of the variation in the environment (Alvarez, 2011; Cohen et al., 2016).

On the other hand, consistent with the argument that more information is represented than can be reported, there is considerable evidence of detailed representations of various properties. For example, a key demonstration comes from Sperling's (1960) famous investigations of what he called iconic memory. Sperling found that observers could report only three to four items within a briefly presented matrix of sixteen letters (in the 'full report' condition). But interestingly, they could also report three to four items from any row that was cued once the array had disappeared, but only if the cue appeared within a very limited time period (around 500 ms; in the 'partial report' condition). This result has been taken to support the overflow argument as it shows that what can be accessed with the 'full report' is more limited than what is represented (as shown by the 'partial report' results). Furthermore, as argued by Haun et al. (2017), there are potentially many more aspects of these displays that can be represented and reported by observers (e.g., the arrangement of letters, the uniformity of spacing between them, their colours, etc.). In line with this, an interesting finding was reported by Bronfman et al. (2014). They tested sensitivity to colour diversity in cued and uncued rows in a Sperling-like briefly presented array. Their observers were able to estimate colour diversity of non-cued arrays without a cost and they argued from this that colour diversity is represented automatically, outside the focus attention, again suggesting that observers perceive more information in the display than what is reported in the 'full report' condition indicates. However, in a later study, Jackson-Nielsen et al. (2017) showed that if observers do not expect a colour diversity judgment, a significant part of them (50% to 80%) cannot correctly determine in a surprise test, how much colour diversity the previous stimulus had. Furthermore, they found that performance on the letter memory task decreases when the observers start expecting the colour diversity task, that is, there are double-task costs. The debate about the interpretation of this and other related findings is still ongoing (Hawkins et al., 2022; Usher et al., 2018) but it seems that at least some minimal level of attention might be needed to process information on colour diversity.

Interestingly, the key claims that have been made from change blindness and inattentional blindness findings have then also been questioned by studies demonstrating that even though observers might not report the supposedly 'missed' target, they still seem to register it to some extent. A nice example is how Moore and Egeth (1997) followed up on inattentional blindness findings reported by Mack and colleagues (1992). In the original study, Mack et al. had presented a difficult perceptual task on an array of task-irrelevant black and white dots finding that observers did not notice salient patterns in the dots when their attention was otherwise engaged, drawing the conclusion that these items were not represented. But importantly, Moore and Egeth found that even if the patterns could not be explicitly reported this does not necessarily mean that they were not perceived. In a clever manipulation Moore and Egeth found even if the patterns were unnoticed, they still strongly influenced judgments of line length (as in, e.g., the Muller-Lyer and Ponzo illusions). This must be considered strong evidence for overflow arguments since the inaccessible information nevertheless influenced performance.

In a similar vein, Fernandez-Duque and Thornton (2000, 2003; see Mitroff & Simons, 2002 for an alternative view) showed how observers seem to be implicitly aware of changes that they do not notice. They found that when observers had not noticed a change in an array of rectangles, they were nevertheless better than chance at locating the changed item. Observers seemed to be able to detect the locus of the change even if they did not notice the change. Sun et al. (2018) recently also showed that change detection performance underestimates the richness of the representation. They presented brief arrays of multicoloured dots asking observers to report the centroid colour of a subset of relatively homogenous dots. They found evidence for high-capacity representation in the centroid judgement data, while change detection performance on similar arrays resulted in capacity estimates of only around two items. These results show that even when observers fail to report some parts of the scene, they might still represent considerable portions of the scene, and far more of the information than the failures to explicitly report this information seem to indicate. According to the overflow account, perceptual representations are richer than what can be consciously accessed indicates. The findings from change blindness and inattentional blindness might be taken to challenge the overflow idea. But the fact that changes that go unreported can nevertheless influence perception is exactly what the overflow account would predict.

4.1.2 Can Summary Statistics Resolve the Paradox?

In an attempt at resolving this controversy, Cohen et al. (2016) suggested that perhaps the rich impressions of consciousness can be explained by the reliance on summary statistics, arguing that 'a handful of items are perceived with high fidelity, while the remainder of the world is represented as an ensemble statistic' (2016, p. 332). This matches the common claim from within the ensemble learning literature that observers represent means and variance of ensembles because of the severe constraints that are assumed to apply to both attentional and cognitive capacity. As explained in Section 2.3, it is indeed well documented that human observers can extract summary statistical information of specific visual dimensions (such as the average colour of a group of items) and these summaries have been shown to work for a number of different feature dimensions such as size, orientation and spatial position, and then also for higher-level properties, such as faces, emotion, or biological motion (see, e.g., Corbett et al., 2023, for review). In a recent meta-analysis, Whitney & Yamanashi Leib (2018) estimated the number of sampled items from an ensemble to be the square root of the elements in the image (see also Section 3.3.1). A rich detailed representation of a few items and a coarse summary representation of the rest is a compromise between the two stances described in Section 4.1.1 since these summary representations are less detailed than what is attended ('grand illusion') but they are still present ('overflow'). Cohen et al. (2016) concluded by claiming that 'ensemble statistics appear to capture the entirety of perceptual experience (p. 324)'. While we do not necessarily disagree with this claim, the key question becomes what the term *ensemble statistics* encompasses and on this we disagree with Cohen et al., since these representations seem to include far more information than Cohen et al. claim and is in fact typically assumed in standard summary statistics accounts.

On the surface, the central claims of the ensemble literature make sense. A sensible goal for the visual system is to represent enough information but not *too* much because the capacity to represent the information is quite limited as classic findings show. These arguments have been used in claims about how the world is represented and the bottom line in these proposals is that the representations are sparse. As explained in Section 4.1.1, many authors (e.g., Cohen et al., 2016; Lau & Rosenthal, 2011; O'Regan, 1992) have argued that the sparseness of these representations can explain phenomena of inattention that show how observers can miss surprising detail in the visual environment such as change blindness (Rensink et al., 1997) and inattentional blindness (Mack et al., 1992; Most et al., 2001). The claim is that this information is not just missed, but is never represented in the first place, and only a small number of items are processed in detail by the visual system. But are our representations really this sparse? There is indeed plenty of evidence of considerable processing of this information that is considered to be so sparsely represented (Bronfman et al., 2014; Fernandez-Duque & Thornton, 2003; Moore & Egeth, 1997). We can then add to this the evidence of surprisingly detailed processing of unattended information from the feature distribution learning method that we covered in detail in Section 3.2 (Chetverikov et al., 2016; Chetverikov & Kristjánsson, 2022). Those findings are also problematic for accounts such as Cohen et al. (2016) who argue for a weaker version of the grand illusion view that involves that the limited capacity is overcome with summary statistics.

Haun et al. (2017) also took issue with the sparse summary statistics view highlighting that rich detailed visual experience is supported by good evidence from introspective reports and phenomenology (mentioning, among other things, some of the findings discussed in this and the previous sections). They claimed that the methods typically used in ensemble perception studies might lead to misleading results, that sparseness arguments rely too strongly on forced-choice binary responses, and that richer experimental paradigms are needed that go beyond these reductionistic approaches. We suggest here that studies that use the FDL methodology meet this challenge, for the most part.

Haun et al. (2017) also claimed that good psychophysical evidence for rich representations is often unjustly discounted (one common criticism is that they are too introspective, e.g.). One good example that they mention is how colour vision in the periphery is generally underestimated and discounted. For example, Tyler (2015) showed, counter to what is almost 'common knowledge' in the field, that there is considerable colour vision in the periphery when the cortical magnification factor is accounted for. Consistently, Webster and colleagues (2010) measured the change in colour appearance between the visual periphery and the central foveal region. They found that the differences in perceived colour between the fovea and the periphery are much smaller than spectral sensitivity at these locations would predict. Also, Wallis et al. (2016) found surprisingly high sensitivity to deviations from natural appearance (through Gaussian blur or texture synthesis) in the periphery (at 10° from the fovea). It is also important to note that this surprisingly good ability at spotting degradations of images, was however only seen for relatively large patches (5.95°) from the images, that provided *context* about the scenes, but not for small patches (0.74°) that provided little context. Tanrikulu et al. (2020) also found that observers were able to encode some properties of distractor distributions in peripheral vision using the feature distribution learning method. All this shows that peripheral vision may not be as poor or sparse as has often been assumed (see, e.g., Kaunitz et al., 2016).

With respect to ensemble properties, it is also important to keep in mind how the capacity of ensemble perception is assessed. In ensemble statistics studies observers are typically asked to make an explicit report on the ensemble in the form of a 2AFC or a reproduction task. But that is not a task that the visual system generally has to perform. As we have shown in Section 3.2, when ensemble representations are measured with more implicit methods, the results typically show more detailed representations. For example, the quickly expanding feature distribution learning literature shows that the shape of the feature distribution is represented by observers over and above simple statistics, such as means and variances (Chetverikov et al., 2016, 2019; Chetverikov & Kristjánsson, 2022). Crucially, an explicit comparison of explicit and implicit tests provided by Hansmann-Roth et al. (2021) shows that observers fail to report complex ensemble properties during explicit tests but importantly, these properties are nevertheless reflected in the implicit tests. This suggests that the explicit tests of summary statistics underestimate the richness of visual representations, supporting the central claims of the overflow argument and related conceptions.

While coarse statistical summaries cannot account for the results of empirical studies that have accumulated in the last decade, it might well be that the representation of variability in the visual world can be described by accounts that assume that the brain uses more complex sets of image-computable statistics (Balas et al., 2009; Freeman & Simoncelli, 2011; Rosenholtz, 2016, 2020). Such encoding schemes assume that visual representations can be described by using thousands of parameters, a large step from the one or two statistics assumed in ensemble studies. Of course, such complex representations can explain the results of diverse implicit tests of visual variability perception. Still, observers can nevertheless distinguish between images with identical statistical properties (Wallis et al., 2016), which suggests that even such complex models do not fully account for the richness of perceptual experience.

It has been proposed that recurrent processing in brain mechanisms devoted to sensory processing could underlie this more detailed processing (see, e.g., Lamme, 2010), notably in areas that are distinct from, for example, the fronto-parietal attention networks that handle attentional selection and are severely capacity limited. While we are sympathetic to such views, we do not believe that at this point we have the grounds to make strong claims regarding neural mechanisms of the learning that is revealed in FDL studies, for example.

4.1.2.1 Summary of Our Views of Overflow versus Grand Illusion Accounts

In the light of all the claims about sparse representations of visual environments that have been inspired by change blindness and inattentional blindness studies, along with the summary statistics literature, it almost seems like a miracle that we can walk around the environment while speaking on the phone (or even on a video call) and not constantly bump into the things in our environment. Why do we not keep stumbling over all kinds of stimuli blocking our path? The easiest and most straightforward explanation is that this information about these obstacles is processed and represented in some way, but probably not consciously (if we assume that there is actually a precise definition of conscious processing). In fact, mechanisms that enable us to avoid obstacles have no need for being conscious. The proposal of Cohen et al. (2016), for example, is that summaries are generated of the peripheral information in the visual field. But summary representations simply do not seem to be up to the job. To take one particular example, summary representations would not allow us to avoid for example the concrete poles often placed on the sidewalk to block cars from entering. The poles should simply be summarized as grey stuff blended with the similarly coloured asphalt on the sidewalk in a summary statistic. But we typically do not stumble on such obstacles even when our attention is focused on something unrelated (although this can sometimes spectacularly fail; but the fact is that *most of the time* it does not).

So we claim that far more information is represented than proponents of the 'grand illusion' accounts propose, and more than just simple summaries. Cohen et al. (2016) posited that overflow arguments must be supported by 'specific examples of visual input that can be consciously perceived without being attended, held in working memory, reported or used to guide volitional action'. Feature distribution learning satisfies at least the last of these criteria. According to the claims of Cohen et al. (2016), if this is indeed the case, there is then less reason for scientists to be sceptical of claims that 'observers can see more than can be accessed' as they put it (p. 332). Let us also note the increased use of 'no-report' paradigms (see Tsuchiya et al., 2015, for review). One benefit of such paradigms is that they avoid the potential confounding effects of explicit reports. All in all, the studies assessing variability perception suggest that observers indeed see more than could be (explicitly) assessed.

4.2 Probabilistic Perception

A long-standing discussion in the vision literature is whether the brain can build probabilistic models of the visual world (Chetverikov & Kristjánsson, 2022; Fiser et al., 2010; Knill & Pouget, 2004; Lange et al., 2023; Pouget et al., 2000; Rahnev et al., 2021; Rao et al., 2002; Tanrıkulu et al., 2021a; Zemel et al., 1998). Importantly, the term 'probabilistic perception' is often taken to mean uncertainty in the inferences about the feature value for a single stimulus, such as the orientation of a Gabor patch. However, this is only a small part of the general taxonomy of probabilistic and non-probabilistic models (Koblinger et al., 2021).

Studies of perceptual variability offer a different perspective, instead putting forward the question 'is variability represented probabilistically?'. There is a continuum of possible answers to this question. For example, a summary statistics representation that includes the mean and variance of stimulus features can be considered probabilistic since it describes the probability of stimulus features approximated with a normal distribution. However, an accurate probabilistic representation would necessarily go beyond just means and variances to represent the distribution of visual features as precisely as possible.

The results from the feature distribution learning literature indicate that perception is inherently probabilistic. Tanrikulu et al. (2021a) speculated that 'the crucial aspect of FDL is that the response feature differs from the visual feature being investigated. Therefore, FDL involves i) no query, ii) no perceptual decision about the distractor features that are learned, iii) no imposition of cognitive categories, iv) no sampling and v) no subjective guessing about the relevant visual feature' (p. 4). This indirect connection enables researchers to sidestep many criticisms that have been used against experiments that have been aimed at assessing probabilistic representations (Block, 2018; Rahnev, 2017). Tanrikulu et al. go on to say: '. . . the probability distributions revealed by the FDL method are not imposed onto the task by the experimenter via a probabilistic description of observer's responses, because the method does not require a response concerning the visual feature whose distribution is being assessed. Instead, these probability distributions originate from the visual process necessary to perform the search' (p. 5).

Chetverikov and Kristjánsson (2022) formalized these arguments in a Bayesian observer model showing how a probabilistic representation of distractor features in FDL studies is related to response times (Figure 4B). In brief, they assumed that the observer obtains noisy sensory samples from each stimulus at each moment in time during the search task. These samples are then used to compare the probability that a stimulus at a given location is a distractor against the probability that it is a target. The decision to report the item at a given location as a target is made when the ratio of the two probabilities (the decision variable) exceeds a threshold value. The observer is assumed to know the sensory noise properties and has learned from preceding trials some information (not necessarily precise) about the probability distributions of target and distractor features. This knowledge and the sensory samples are used to compute the decision variable. Crucially, the model demonstrated that there is a monotonic relationship between the expected probability that a certain feature value corresponds to a distracting stimulus and the response times on test trial when the target has that particular feature value (see Chetverikov and Kristjánsson, 2022, for details). In other words, the higher the probability that a certain orientation is a distractor, the slower the search would be when this feature belongs to a target instead. This formally proves that response times in FDL can be used to approximately reconstruct distractor representations, once again demonstrating how observers have detailed probabilistic representations of distracting stimuli.

Notably, both explicit and implicit tests can be united in a probabilistic perception framework. For example, Utochkin et al. (2023) implement a noisy observer model using neural population codes and showed that this implementation can explain the results for both implicit and explicit tasks. However, for reasons outlined in Section 3.3 we believe that there is currently little empirical support for the idea that the same mechanisms subserve responses in both these types of task. Thus, while they could be explained by a single probabilistic model, it does not seem to be the case that such an explanation would be able to account for the diverging patterns of findings related to explicit and implicit tasks.

4.3 The Nature of Target Templates and Templates for Rejection

In the visual search literature, search performance is often described as reflecting the operation of target and distractor templates, that is, the representations of these items held in memory (Desimone & Duncan, 1995). Specifically, target templates serve the purpose of filtering relevant information and/or checking that the attended stimulus is a target, while filtering of irrelevant information is thought to be based on distractor templates tuned to specific feature values that are to be ignored (have been also called 'templates for rejection', see Arita et al., 2012; Woodman et al., 2013, for review). These templates have traditionally been thought to match exactly the features of targets or distractors, perhaps with the addition of some noise. However, in the light of what is now known about the way our visual system represents the variability of stimuli features, it might be more appropriate to consider them as approximations of feature distributions of targets and distractors.

Kristjánsson (2022) made the case that the nature of the representations that we build up internally during exposure to the environment are probabilistic, citing evidence obtained with the FDL method. Another claim that follows from that one is that various priming effects such as for colour (Maljkovic & Nakayama, 1994), orientation (Huang et al., 2004; Kristjánsson et al., 2002), or other features simply boil down to the learning of a distribution with no variance (see also Chetverikov et al., 2017a).

Geng and colleagues have also reported evidence that is consistent with this. For example, Geng et al. (2017) showed that perceptual and attentional history plays a key role in the strategic biasing of attentional templates. In their study, the probability that a distractor was similar to the target influenced search template tuning. If a template is just the target feature value plus noise, then it should be the same regardless of distractor identity. However, Geng et al. showed how increased similarity of the search items led to more precisely tuned templates. The results of Hansmann-Roth et al. (2022) then show how this tuning process may lead to increasingly precise representations of the distributions that targets are drawn from (see also Chapman et al., 2023).

In Won and Geng (2018), observers searched for a grey square among coloured squares. During a training session, the distractors were always drawn from the same set of coloured distractors. When new distractors were introduced, the distance in feature space of these new distractors from the old ones determined how much suppression they received. Won and Geng argued that the templates of the distractors from the training phases have broad tuning, allowing suppression of new items, that are similar, but not identical, to the learned ones and that target templates require sharper tuning (similar to what Chetverikov et al., 2020, argued). Lau et al. (2021) studied a similar problem, using real images instead of the simpler stimuli used in the previously mentioned studies. They reported that target template tuning is coarse when targets and distractors can easily be distinguished (e.g., man-made objects versus animals) but when the target template needs to be more detailed (e.g., within-category search), these learned templates do not transfer well.

Chetverikov et al. (2020) investigated whether instead of reflecting specific values, such rejection can be probabilistic, or more specifically, whether the rejection templates are probabilistic, and how accurately such templates reflect the probabilities of features to be ignored (as they are being learned). Using a double-target search task combined with a bimodal distractor distribution on the learning trials, they found that both modes of the distractor feature distribution are represented on a trial-by-trial basis. This would be impossible if only the variance of distractors were taken into account in the template formation. Instead, the results suggest that rejection templates are probabilistic.

As Won and Geng (2018) argue, distractor templates are more broadly tuned than target templates. This could be an efficient strategy for the visual system since it may allow easy generalization of suppression of a distractor *range*, a strategy that might not be as useful to find targets. For targets, a broad representation could, for example, lead to high numbers of false alarms. To take one example, Geng et al. (2017) observed that when targets are similar to distractors, templates are sharpened and shifted away from distractors. They showed how the probability that a distractor is similar to the target affects the tuning of search templates. The increased similarity of targets and distractors led to the more precise tuning of the templates. This is reminiscent of findings that indicate that templates can be strategically biased away from the actual values of targets for maximum discriminability (Navalpakkam & Itti, 2007; Scolari & Serences, 2009; Yu & Geng, 2019), if this provides the best way of distinguishing targets from distractors. Alternatively, such biases could be a side effect of an attempt to disentangle a mixture of sensory signals related to distractors and targets in working memory, similar to other inter-item or contextual effects in memory and perception (Chetverikov, 2023).

Further cementing the role of history in generating selection preferences in visual attention tasks, observers seem to *predict* future stimuli based on past statistics that they have tracked over a set of adjacent trials – they represent what the target is likely to look like given the previous history (Witkowski & Geng, 2022). In this case, the most reliable predictor was the progression throughout history. Note that this is consistent with proposals that the visual system prioritizes stable features over variable ones (see, e.g., Witkowski & Geng, 2019). While this is consistent with the Bayesian principles discussed in Section 4.2, integration of previously perceived stimuli is clearly not always Bayesian optimal (see further discussion in the next section).

This meshes well with recent results from Yoo et al. (2021) who showed how uncertainty is *actively* represented in working memory. Many estimates of working memory capacity describe it as a single number, but the assumption has also been that the estimates of the number (representing capacity) can be noisy. Yoo et al. used an orientation change detection task and contrasted performance when observers were required to maintain the uncertainty in memory and when the uncertainty was available in the test image. In the former case, they found evidence that the uncertainty was maintained during the test period and as Yoo et al. argued, this use was implicit since the representation of uncertainty wasn't an actual requirement of the task.

4.4 Inferences in the Presence of Variability

Having discussed the empirical findings on the effects of variability and its representation, how should we understand these findings at a theoretical level? A leading theoretical approach in modern perception science is the idea of predictive coding (Rao & Ballard, 1999), often framed as a Bayesian inference process (Friston, 2010). Bayesian models of perception have taken centre stage in explaining the effects of stimulus variability at different timescales (Seriès & Seitz, 2013), such as in studies of cardinal priors in orientation perception (Bertana et al., 2021; Girshick et al., 2011). This is not surprising since variability is tightly related to uncertainty that plays a central role in the idea of Bayesian or, more generally, probabilistic perception (Koblinger et al., 2021; Ma, 2012; Pouget et al., 2013; van Bergen et al., 2015). We will discuss the role of variability within the general framework of probabilistic perception and whether simpler, non-probabilistic models, can explain the existing body of research.

One of the most straightforward predictions of Bayesian accounts of perception is that when information from multiple sources is integrated, the estimated stimulus value should be equal to the weighted sum of the sources' values with weights provided by the precision of the sources (see Ma et al., 2023, for an introduction on Bayesian models of perception). For example, when an observer sees a flash and hears a sound corresponding to the same stimulus, the estimated location of that stimulus would be between the location of the flash and location of the sounds. Usually, visual estimates of location are more precise and hence the estimated location would be closer to the flash than to the sound. Variability affects the uncertainty in estimates of the stimulus mean value (see Section 1.3 and Figure 2 for the difference between uncertainty and variability), so when the information about two stimuli that have variable features is integrated, the result of this integration should be affected by the variability of each stimulus.

Notably, however, empirical studies have provided little support for such simple Bayesian accounts. For example, serial dependence in vision is a well-known example of how information might be integrated across trials (Fischer & Whitney, 2014; see Pascucci et al., 2023 for a review). When observers estimate the features (e.g., orientation) of stimuli, their responses on trial N are typically attracted towards stimuli on trial N-1. This has also been observed when participants are required to estimate the mean of a visual ensemble (Manassi et al., 2017). Importantly, in the current context, Son and colleagues (2021) studied how variability in a visual ensemble affects the mean estimates in sequential decisions. Under a simple Bayesian account, judgments of a stimulus with higher uncertainty should be biased more towards the preceding stimulus with lower uncertainty compared to the opposite case (van Bergen & Jehee, 2019). What Son et al. found, however, was that the low-variability stimulus created a repulsive bias in the perceptual judgments of the subsequent high-variability stimulus (while the attraction was observed in the opposite case). The authors explained their results by a more complex and suboptimal model than straightforward Bayesian models, which combines Bayesian integration with changes to sensory noise due to adaptation (see also Wei & Stocker, 2015). Notably, such a pattern of results can be explained with optimal models that use different assumptions (Chetverikov, 2023). However, the effects of variability on biases in sequential decisions clearly cannot be accounted for by a simple Bayesian model.

Tanrikulu et al. (2021b) tested what we call the straightforward Bayesian account differently. They presented distributions with low versus high variance alternatively during learning trials in an FDL paradigm, predicting that the low variance distributions would be weighted more highly on the test trials. In three experiments Tanrikulu et al. found instead that by far the highest weight was assigned to the most recent distractor distribution (on the most recent trial), irrespective of variance. There was also very little, if any, integration of information from the two learning distributions. The response time curves from the test trials (reflecting the role-reversal effects, as explained in section 3.2) were simply determined by the variance on the last learning trial. This showed how information integration across trials is dominated by a strong recency effect. Tanrikulu et al. speculated that there may have simply been too much variability in the stimulus history for the visual system to weigh anything else than the most recent input highly. This result also contradicts the simple Bayesian observer account.

To reiterate, more complex models may still be able to accommodate the data. For example, Tanrikulu et al. (2021b) suggested that the ability to pick up distractor statistics could be limited because the distributions were unstable from one trial to the next. Such instability can be taken into account in models involving causal inference similar to multisensory perception (e.g., Körding et al., 2007). The notion of optimality can also change when time and resource constraints are taken into account (e.g., Vul et al., 2014). Alternatively, suboptimal heuristic models can be used to explain the effect of variability on inferences (see Rahnev & Denison, 2018 for a general discussion on optimality in perception). For example, it may be possible to take only a rough estimate of how variable the stimulus is and the small differences in the experimental design in Tanrikulu et al. (2021b) may not be strong enough to create noticeable effects, resulting in the dominance of the most recent stimulus. Similar conclusions regarding recency effects have been reached by Raviv, Ahissar & Loewenstein (2012) who used a two-tone discrimination task. A better theoretical account of how perceptual information is integrated may assume that vision is simply totally opportunistic in terms of the information that the system uses and that under conditions of high uncertainty a recency effect is induced, instead of an optimally integrated representation.

4.5 Summary and Concluding Remarks

Our aim in this Element has been to assess how variability affects performance in visual tasks and how variability is represented by human observers. Our central argument can be summarized in the following statements:

1) Variability in visual stimuli affects performance in a wide range of tasks, and this influence is not always negative.

2) The brain represents the variability in the visual environment at a much higher level of detail than the recent consensus in the literature seems to suggest.

3) There is evidence that variability could be represented as a specific entity, not just as a characteristic of the particular stimuli in each case, but this may vary by task demands.

4) Reliance on explicit reports for understanding how variability is represented has underestimated the capacity for storing information about variability. Variability is not represented so that it can be used for explicit forced choice or adjustment tasks – it is represented for interacting with the world.

5) Explicit tests may force observers into a low-dimensional response space, that is sparser than what they have available for action.

6) Tests that tap into how representations may be used for interactions, such as the implicit tests in the *feature distribution learning* (FDL) method, may be better suited to assessing how variability is represented.

7) Arguments that the apparent detail in the visual environment is illusory may rely on the untested assumption that what is represented can be reported.

8) A natural conclusion is that more is represented than can be consciously accessed and reported – there is considerable 'overflow' in other words.

The world is full of detail and our visual system can represent far more of this detail than is often assumed. Here we have highlighted how vision scientists are beginning to understand how representations of environmental variability are constructed. The evidence strongly suggests that these representations are implicit and cannot easily be accessed with explicit reports that may force observers into lower-dimensional spaces of possibilities than those used for interactions with the world. Importantly, our analysis also helps us with differentiating between probabilistic and non-probabilistic models of perception since some of the most important experimental paradigms that we have reviewed provide much richer data than traditional studies with more impoverished stimuli. It is also essential to highlight that representations of variability can be very useful, allowing us to successfully move around, and interact with our perceptual environment. Importantly, for such interactions, there is no need for this information to be conscious.

The findings of Hansmann-Roth et al. (2021) where large differences were observed between explicit and implicit reports of distribution properties highlight that different tasks might require different inferences while perception is the same. The importance of this is that the capacity for representation used for action may be severely underestimated. Sparse representation views have been all the rage for a quarter century, now. While it is almost certainly true that summaries of information can be generated when observers are specifically asked about this, the question remains of to what degree such findings could be reflecting the task rather than perception *per se*. When observers are asked to summarize information, they can do so. But is this the *basis* for perception and action? Does the fact that observers can do this mean that the information is represented in this way? This is what we doubt. The information for perception within the world and action within the visual environment seems to be far richer than this suggests, reflecting the detail in our visual representations.

References

Acerbi, L., Wolpert, D. M., & Vijayakumar, S. (2012). Internal representations of temporal statistics and feedback calibrate motor-sensory interval timing. *PLOS Computational Biology, 8*(11), e1002771. https://doi.org/10.1371/jour nal.pcbi.1002771.

Alvarez, G. A. (2011). Representing multiple objects as an ensemble enhances visual cognition. *Trends in Cognitive Sciences, 15*(3), 122–131. https://doi .org/10.1016/j.tics.2011.01.003.

Arita, J. T., Carlisle, N. B., & Woodman, G. F. (2012). Templates for rejection: Configuring attention to ignore task-irrelevant features. *Journal of Experimental Psychology: Human Perception and Performance, 38*(3), 580–584. https://doi .org/10.1037/a0027885.

Atchley, P., & Andersen, G. J. (1995). Discrimination of speed distributions: Sensitivity to statistical properties. *Vision Research, 35*(22), 3131–3144. https://doi.org/10.1016/0042-6989(95)00057-7.

Attarha, M., & Moore, C. M. (2015). The capacity limitations of orientation summary statistics. *Attention, Perception, & Psychophysics, 77*(4), 1116–1131. https://doi.org/10.3758/s13414-015-0870-0.

Attarha, M., Moore, C. M., & Vecera, S. P. (2014). Summary statistics of size: Fixed processing capacity for multiple ensembles but unlimited processing capacity for single ensembles. *Journal of Experimental Psychology: Human Perception and Performance, 40*(4), 1440–1449. https://doi.org/10.1037/ a0036206.

Avraham, T., Yeshurun, Y., Lindenbaum, M., Yeshurun, Y., & Lindenbaum, M. (2008). Predicting visual search performance by quantifying stimuli similarities. *Journal of Vision, 8*(2008), 9.1–22. https://doi.org/10.1167/8.4.9.

Balas, B. J., Nakano, L., & Rosenholtz, R. (2009). A summary-statistic repre- sentation in peripheral vision explains visual crowding. *Journal of Vision, 9* (12), 13.1–18. https://doi.org/10.1167/9.12.13.

Bauer, B. (2015). A selective summary of visual averaging research and issues up to 2000. *Journal of Vision, 15*(4), 1–15. https://doi.org/10.1167/15.4.14.

Bays, P., Schneegans, S., Ma, W. J., & Brady, T. (2022). *Representation and computation in working memory.* PsyArXiv. https://doi.org/10.31234/osf.io/ kubr9.

Bertana, A., Chetverikov, A., van Bergen, R. S., Ling, S., & Jehee, J. F. M. (2021). Dual strategies in human confidence judgments. *Journal of Vision, 21* (5), 21. https://doi.org/10.1167/jov.21.5.21.

Biederman, I. (1987). Recognition-by-components: A theory of human image understanding. *Psychological Review, 94*, 115–147. https://doi.org/10.1037/0033-295X.94.2.115.

Block, N. (2011). Perceptual consciousness overflows cognitive access. *Trends in Cognitive Sciences, 15*(12), 1–9. https://doi.org/10.1016/j.tics.2011.11.001.

Block, N. (2018). If perception is probabilistic, why does it not seem probabilistic? *Philosophical Transactions of the Royal Society B: Biological Sciences, 373*(1755). https://doi.org/10.1098/rstb.2017.0341.

Boldt, A., de Gardelle, V., & Yeung, N. (2017). The impact of evidence reliability on sensitivity and bias in decision confidence. *Journal of Experimental Psychology: Human Perception and Performance, 43*(8), 1520–1531. https://doi.org/10.1037/xhp0000404.

Braddick, O. J., O'Brien, J. M. D., Wattam-Bell, J. et al. (2001). Brain areas sensitive to coherent visual motion. *Perception, 30*(1), 61–72. https://doi.org/10.1068/p3048.

Brady, T. F., & Alvarez, G. A. (2011). Hierarchical encoding in visual working memory ensemble statistics bias memory for individual items. *Psychological Science, 22*(3), 384–392. https://doi.org/10.1177/0956797610397956.

Bravo, M. J., & Nakayama, K. (1992). The role of attention in different visual-search tasks. *Perception & Psychophysics, 51*(5), 465–472. https://doi.org/10.3758/BF03211642.

Bronfman, Z. Z., Brezis, N., Jacobson, H., & Usher, M. (2014). We see more than we can report: 'cost free' color phenomenality outside focal attention. *Psychological Science, 25*(7), 1394–1403. https://doi.org/10.1177/0956797614532656.

Calder-Travis, J., & Ma, W. J. (2020). Explaining the effects of distractor statistics in visual search. *Journal of Vision, 20*(13), 11. https://doi.org/10.1167/jov.20.13.11.

Cha, O., Blake, R., & Gauthier, I. (2022). Contribution of a common ability in average and variability judgments. *Psychonomic Bulletin & Review, 29*(1), 108–115. https://doi.org/10.3758/s13423-021-01982-1.

Chapman, A. F., Chunharas, C., & Störmer, V. S. (2023). Feature-based attention warps the perception of visual features. *Scientific Reports, 13*(1), Article 1. https://doi.org/10.1038/s41598-023-33488-2.

Chetverikov, A. (2023). *Demixing model: A normative explanation for inter-item biases in memory and perception.* bioRxiv. https://doi.org/10.1101/2023.03.26.534226.

Chetverikov, A., Campana, G., & Kristjánsson, Á. (2016). Building ensemble representations: How the shape of preceding distractor distributions affects visual search. *Cognition*, *153*, 196–210. https://doi.org/10.1016/j.cognition.2016.04.018.

Chetverikov, A., Campana, G., & Kristjánsson, Á. (2017a). Learning features in a complex and changing environment: A distribution-based framework for visual attention and vision in general. In Christina J. Howard (Ed.), *Progress in Brain Research* (Vol. 236, pp. 97–120). Elsevier. https://doi.org/10.1016/bs.pbr.2017.07.001.

Chetverikov, A., Campana, G., & Kristjánsson, Á. (2017b). Rapid learning of visual ensembles. *Journal of Vision*, *17*(21), 1–15. https://doi.org/10.1167/17.2.21.

Chetverikov, A., Campana, G., & Kristjánsson, Á. (2017c). Representing color ensembles. *Psychological Science*, *28*(10), 1–8. https://doi.org/10.1177/0956797617713787.

Chetverikov, A., Campana, G., & Kristjánsson, Á. (2017d). Set size manipulations reveal the boundary conditions of distractor distribution learning. *Vision Research*, *140*(November), 144–156. https://doi.org/10.1016/j.visres.2017.08.003.

Chetverikov, A., Campana, G., & Kristjánsson, Á. (2020). Probabilistic rejection templates in visual working memory. *Cognition*, *196*, 104075. https://doi.org/10.1016/j.cognition.2019.104075.

Chetverikov, A., Hansmann-Roth, S., Tanrikulu, Ö. D., & Kristjánsson, Á. (2019). Feature distribution learning (FDL): A new method for studying visual ensembles perception with priming of attention shifts. In Pollmann, S. (Ed.), *Neuromethods* (pp. 1–21). Springer. https://doi.org/10.1007/7657_2019_20.

Chetverikov, A., & Jehee, J. F. M. (2023). Motion direction is represented as a bimodal probability distribution in the human visual cortex. *Nature Communications*, 14(7634), Article 1. https://doi.org/10.1038/s41467-023-43251-w.

Chetverikov, A., & Kristjánsson, Á. (2015). History effects in visual search for monsters: Search times, choice biases, and liking. *Attention, Perception, & Psychophysics*, *77*(2), 402–412. https://doi.org/10.3758/s13414-014-0782-4.

Chetverikov, A., & Kristjánsson, A. (2022). Probabilistic representations as building blocks for higher-level vision. *Neurons, Behavior, Data Analysis, and Theory*, 1–32. https://doi.org/10.51628/001c.24910.

Chong, S. C., & Treisman, A. (2003). Representation of statistical properties. *Vision Research*, *43*(4), 393–404. https://doi.org/10.1016/S0042-6989(02)00596-5.

Cohen, M. A., Dennett, D. C., & Kanwisher, N. (2016). What is the bandwidth of perceptual experience? *Trends in Cognitive Sciences*, *20*(5), 324–335. https://doi.org/10.1016/j.tics.2016.03.006.

Corbett, J. E., & Melcher, D. (2014). Stable statistical representations facilitate visual search. *Journal of Experimental Psychology: Human Perception and Performance*, *40*(5), 1915–1925. https://doi.org/10.1037/a0037375.

Corbett, J. E., Utochkin, I., & Hochstein, S. (2023). *The Pervasiveness of Ensemble Perception: Not Just Your Average Review.* Cambridge University Press. https://doi.org/10.1017/9781009222716.

Corpuz, R. L., & Oriet, C. (2022). Within-person variability contributes to more durable learning of faces. *Canadian Journal of Experimental Psychology / Revue Canadienne de Psychologie Expérimentale*, *76*(4), 270–282. https://doi.org/10.1037/cep0000282.

Dakin, S. C. (2001). Information limit on the spatial integration of local orientation signals. *Journal of the Optical Society of America A*, *18*(5), 1016–1026. https://doi.org/10.1364/JOSAA.18.001016.

Dakin, S. C., & Watt, R. J. J. (1997). The computation of orientation statistics from visual texture. *Vision Research*, *37*(22), 3181–3192. https://doi.org/10.1016/S0042-6989(97)00133-8.

Danckert, J., & Goodale, M. A. (2000). Blindsight: A conscious route to unconscious vision. *Current Biology*, *10*(2), R64–R67. https://doi.org/10.1016/S0960-9822(00)00284-0.

Daniels, D. P., Neale, M. A., & Greer, L. L. (2017). Spillover bias in diversity judgment. *Organizational Behavior and Human Decision Processes*, *139*, 92–105. https://doi.org/10.1016/j.obhdp.2016.12.005.

Desimone, R., & Duncan, J. (1995). Neural mechanisms of selective visual attention. *Annual Review of Neuroscience*, *18*, 193–222. https://doi.org/10.1146/annurev.ne.18.030195.001205.

Driver, J., McLeod, P., & Dienes, Z. (1992). Motion coherence and conjunction search: Implications for guided search theory. *Perception & Psychophysics*, *51*(1), 79–85. https://doi.org/10.3758/BF03205076.

Duncan, J., & Humphreys, G. W. (1989). Visual search and stimulus similarity. *Psychological Review*, *96*(3), 433–458. https://doi.org/10.1037/0033-295x.96.3.433.

Fahle, M. (2005). Perceptual learning: Specificity versus generalization. *Current Opinion in Neurobiology*, *15*(2), 154–160. https://doi.org/10.1016/j.conb.2005.03.010.

Failing, M., & Theeuwes, J. (2018). Selection history: How reward modulates selectivity of visual attention. *Psychonomic Bulletin & Review*, *25*(2), 514–538. https://doi.org/10.3758/s13423-017-1380-y.

Fechner, G. (1860). *Elements of Psychophysics. Vol. I*. New York.

Fernandez-Duque, D., & Thornton, I. M. (2000). Change detection without awareness: Do explicit reports underestimate the representation of change in the visual system? *Visual Cognition, 7*(1–3), 323–344. https://doi.org/10.1080/135062800394838.

Fernandez-Duque, D., & Thornton, I. M. (2003). Explicit mechanisms do not account for implicit localization and identification of change: An empirical reply to Mitroff et al. (2002). *Journal of Experimental Psychology: Human Perception and Performance, 29*(5), 846–858. https://doi.org/10.1037/0096-1523.29.5.846.

Fischer, J., & Whitney, D. (2014). Serial dependence in visual perception. *Nature Neuroscience, 17*(5), 738–743. https://doi.org/10.1038/nn.3689.

Fiser, J., Berkes, P., Orbán, G., & Lengyel, M. (2010). Statistically optimal perception and learning: From behavior to neural representations. *Trends in Cognitive Sciences, 14*(3), 119–130. https://doi.org/10.1016/j.tics.2010.01.003.

Freeman, J., & Simoncelli, E. P. (2011). Metamers of the ventral stream. *Nature Neuroscience, 14*(9), 1195–1201. https://doi.org/10.1038/nn.2889.

Friston, K. J. (2010). The free-energy principle: A unified brain theory? *Nature Reviews Neuroscience, 11*(2), 127–138. https://doi.org/10.1038/nrn2787.

Gao, Y., Xue, K., Odegaard, B., & Rahnev, D. (2023). *Common computations in automatic cue combination and metacognitive confidence reports* (p. 2023.06.07.544029). bioRxiv. https://doi.org/10.1101/2023.06.07.544029.

Geng, J. J., DiQuattro, N. E., & Helm, J. (2017). Distractor probability changes the shape of the attentional template. *Journal of Experimental Psychology: Human Perception and Performance, 43*(12), 1993–2007. https://doi.org/10.1037/xhp0000430.

Gibson, J. J. (1950). *The Perception of the Visual World* (pp. xii, 242). Houghton Mifflin.

Gibson, J. J. (1962). Observations on active touch. *Psychological Review, 69*(6), 477–491. https://doi.org/10.1037/h0046962.

Girshick, A. R., Landy, M. S., & Simoncelli, E. P. (2011). Cardinal rules: Visual orientation perception reflects knowledge of environmental statistics. *Nature Neuroscience, 14*(7), 926–932. https://doi.org/10.1038/nn.2831.

Gold, J. I., & Watanabe, T. (2010). Perceptual learning. *Current Biology, 20*(2), R46–R48. https://doi.org/10.1016/j.cub.2009.10.066.

Goodale, M. A., & Milner, A. D. (1992). Separate visual pathways for perception and action. *Trends in Neurosciences, 15*(1), 20–25. https://doi.org/10.1016/0166-2236(92)90344-8.

Haberman, J., Brady, T. F., & Alvarez, G. A. (2015a). Individual differences in ensemble perception reveal multiple, independent levels of ensemble representation. *Journal of Experimental Psychology: General, 144*(2), 432–446. https://doi.org/10.1037/xge0000053.

Haberman, J., Lee, P., & Whitney, D. (2015b). Mixed emotions: Sensitivity to facial variance in a crowd of faces. *Journal of Vision, 15*(4), 16. https://doi .org/10.1167/15.4.16.

Haberman, J., & Whitney, D. (2011). Efficient summary statistical representation when change localization fails. *Psychonomic Bulletin & Review, 18*(5), 855–859. https://doi.org/10.3758/s13423-011-0125-6.

Haberman, J., & Whitney, D. (2012). Ensemble perception: Summarizing the scene and broadening the limits of visual processing. In J. M. Wolfe & L. Robertson (Eds.), *From Perception to Consciousness: Searching with Anne Treisman* (pp. 339–349). Oxford University Press.

Hansmann-Roth, S., Chetverikov, A., & Kristjánsson, Á. (2019). Representing color and orientation ensembles: Can observers learn multiple feature distributions? *Journal of Vision, 19*(9), 1–17. https://doi.org/10.1167/19.9.2.

Hansmann-Roth, S., Chetverikov, A., & Kristjánsson, Á. (2023). Extracting statistical information about shapes in the visual environment. *Vision Research, 206*, 108190. https://doi.org/10.1016/j.visres.2023.108190.

Hansmann-Roth, S., Kristjánsson, Á., Whitney, D., & Chetverikov, A. (2021). Dissociating implicit and explicit ensemble representations reveals the limits of visual perception and the richness of behavior. *Scientific Reports, 11*, 3899. https://doi.org/10.1038/s41598-021-83358-y.

Hansmann-Roth, S., Þorsteinsdóttir, S., Geng, J. J., & Kristjánsson, Á. (2022). Temporal integration of feature probability distributions. *Psychological Research, 86*, 2030–2044. https://doi.org/10.1007/s00426-021-01621-3.

Harrison, W. J., McMaster, J. M. V., & Bays, P. M. (2021). Limited memory for ensemble statistics in visual change detection. *Cognition, 214*, 104763. https://doi.org/10.1016/j.cognition.2021.104763.

Haun, A. M., Tononi, G., Koch, C., & Tsuchiya, N. (2017). Are we underestimating the richness of visual experience? *Neuroscience of Consciousness, 2017*(1), niw023. https://doi.org/10.1093/nc/niw023.

Hawkins, B., Evans, D., Preston, A. et al. (2022). Color diversity judgments in peripheral vision: Evidence against 'cost-free' representations. *PLOS ONE, 17*(12), e0279686. https://doi.org/10.1371/journal.pone.0279686.

Hebart, M. N., Donner, T. H., & Haynes, J. D. (2012). Human visual and parietal cortex encode visual choices independent of motor plans. *NeuroImage, 63*(3), 1393–1403. https://doi.org/10.1016/j.neuroimage.2012.08.027.

Hecht, S., Shlaer, S., & Pirenne, M. H. (1942). Energy, quanta, and vision. *Journal of General Physiology, 25*(6), 819–840. https://doi.org/10.1085/ jgp.25.6.819.

Herce Castañón, S., Moran, R., Ding, J. et al. (2019). Human noise blindness drives suboptimal cognitive inference. *Nature Communications*, *10*(1), 1719. https://doi.org/10.1038/s41467-019-09330-7.

Higuchi, Y., Ueda, Y., Shibata, K., & Saiki, J. (2020). Spatial variability induces generalization in contextual cueing. *Journal of Experimental Psychology: Learning, Memory, and Cognition*, *46*(12), 2295–2313. https://doi.org/10.1037/xlm0000796.

Hochstein, S., Pavlovskaya, M., Bonneh, Y. S., & Soroker, N. (2018). Comparing set summary statistics and outlier pop out in vision. *Journal of Vision*, *18*(13), 12. https://doi.org/10.1167/18.13.12.

Hoffman, D. D., & Richards, W. A. (1984). Parts of recognition. *Cognition*, *18*(1), 65–96. https://doi.org/10.1016/0010-0277(84)90022-2.

Huang, L., Holcombe, A. O., & Pashler, H. (2004). Repetition priming in visual search: Episodic retrieval, not feature priming. *Memory & Cognition*, *32*(1), 12–20.

Hussain, Z., Bennett, P. J., & Sekuler, A. B. (2012). Versatile perceptual learning of textures after variable exposures. *Vision Research*, *61*, 89–94. https://doi.org/10.1016/j.visres.2012.01.005.

Iakovlev, A. U., & Utochkin, I. S. (2021). Roles of saliency and set size in ensemble averaging. *Attention, Perception, & Psychophysics*, *83*(3), 1251–1262. https://doi.org/10.3758/s13414-020-02089-w.

Iakovlev, A. U., & Utochkin, I. S. (2023). Ensemble averaging: What can we learn from skewed feature distributions? *Journal of Vision*, *23*(1), 5. https://doi.org/10.1167/jov.23.1.5.

Im, H. Y., & Halberda, J. (2013). The effects of sampling and internal noise on the representation of ensemble average size. *Attention, Perception, & Psychophysics*, *75*(2), 278–286. https://doi.org/10.3758/s13414-012-0399-4.

Im, H. Y., Tiurina, N. A., & Utochkin, I. S. (2020). An explicit investigation of the roles that feature distributions play in rapid visual categorization. *Attention, Perception, and Psychophysics*, *83*, 1050–1069. https://doi.org/10.3758/s13414-020-02046-7.

Jackson-Nielsen, M., Cohen, M. A., & Pitts, M. A. (2017). Perception of ensemble statistics requires attention. *Consciousness and Cognition*, *48*, 149–160. https://doi.org/10.1016/j.concog.2016.11.007.

Jeong, J., & Chong, S. C. (2020). Adaptation to mean and variance: Interrelationships between mean and variance representations in orientation perception. *Vision Research*, *167*, 46–53. https://doi.org/10.1016/j.visres.2020.01.002.

Jeong, J., & Chong, S. C. (2021). Perceived variability reflects the reliability of individual items. *Vision Research, 183*, 91–105. https://doi.org/10.1016/j.visres.2021.02.008.

Kanaya, S., Hayashi, M. J., & Whitney, D. (2018). Exaggerated groups: Amplification in ensemble coding of temporal and spatial features. *Proceedings of the Royal Society B: Biological Sciences, 285*(1879), 20172770. https://doi.org/10.1098/rspb.2017.2770.

Karni, A., & Sagi, D. (1991). Where practice makes perfect in texture discrimination: Evidence for primary visual cortex plasticity. *Proceedings of the National Academy of Sciences, 88*(11), 4966–4970. https://doi.org/10.1073/pnas.88.11.4966.

Kaunitz, L. N., Rowe, E. G., & Tsuchiya, N. (2016). Large capacity of conscious access for incidental memories in natural scenes. *Psychological Science, 27*(9), 1266–1277. https://doi.org/10.1177/0956797616658869.

Kay, K., Bonnen, K., Denison, R. N., Arcaro, M. J., & Barack, D. L. (2023). Tasks and their role in visual neuroscience. *Neuron, 111*(11), 1697–1713. https://doi.org/10.1016/j.neuron.2023.03.022.

Khayat, N., & Hochstein, S. (2018). Perceiving set mean and range: Automaticity and precision. *Journal of Vision, 18*(9), 23. https://doi.org/10.1167/18.9.23.

Khayat, N., & Hochstein, S. (2019). Relating categorization to set summary statistics perception. *Attention, Perception, & Psychophysics, 81*(8), 2850–2872. https://doi.org/10.3758/s13414-019-01792-7.

Khvostov, V. A., & Utochkin, I. S. (2019). Independent and parallel visual processing of ensemble statistics: Evidence from dual tasks. *Journal of Vision, 19*(9), 1–18. https://doi.org/10.1167/19.9.3.

Kim, M., & Chong, S. C. (2020). The visual system does not compute a single mean but summarizes a distribution. *Journal of Experimental Psychology: Human Perception and Performance, 46*(9), 1013–1028. https://doi.org/10.1037/xhp0000804.

Knill, D. C., & Pouget, A. (2004). The Bayesian brain: The role of uncertainty in neural coding and computation. *Trends in Neurosciences, 27*(12), 712–719. https://doi.org/10.1016/j.tins.2004.10.007.

Koblinger, Á., Fiser, J., & Lengyel, M. (2021). Representations of uncertainty: Where art thou? *Current Opinion in Behavioral Sciences, 38*, 150–162. https://doi.org/10.1016/j.cobeha.2021.03.009.

Körding, K. P., Beierholm, U., Ma, W. J. et al. (2007). Causal inference in multisensory perception. *PLoS ONE, 2*(9). e943. https://doi.org/10.1371/journal.pone.0000943.

Kristjánsson, Á. (2022). Priming of probabilistic attentional templates. *Psychonomic Bulletin & Review, 30*, 22–39. https://doi.org/10.3758/s13423-022-02125-w.

Kristjánsson, Á., & Ásgeirsson, Á. G. (2019). Attentional priming: Recent insights and current controversies. *Current Opinion in Psychology, 29*, 71–75. https://doi.org/10.1016/j.copsyc.2018.11.013.

Kristjánsson, Á., & Draschkow, D. (2021). Keeping it real: Looking beyond capacity limits in visual cognition. *Attention, Perception, & Psychophysics, 83*(4), 1375–1390. https://doi.org/10.3758/s13414-021-02256-7.

Kristjánsson, Á., & Driver, J. (2008). Priming in visual search: Separating the effects of target repetition, distractor repetition and role-reversal. *Vision Research, 48*(10), 1217–1232. https://doi.org/10.1016/j.visres.2008.02.007.

Kristjánsson, Á., Vuilleumier, P., Malhotra, P., Husain, M., & Driver, J. (2005). Priming of color and position during visual search in unilateral spatial neglect. *Journal of Cognitive Neuroscience, 17*(6), 859–873. https://doi.org/10.1162/0898929054021148.

Kristjánsson, Á., Wang, D., & Nakayama, K. (2002). The role of priming in conjunctive visual search. *Cognition, 85*(1), 37–52.

Lamme, V. A. F. (2010). How neuroscience will change our view on consciousness. *Cognitive Neuroscience, 1*(3), 204–220. https://doi.org/10.1080/17588921003731586.

Lamy, D. F., Antebi, C., Aviani, N., & Carmel, T. (2008). Priming of pop-out provides reliable measures of target activation and distractor inhibition in selective attention. *Vision Research, 48*(1), 30–41. https://doi.org/10.1016/j.visres.2007.10.009.

Lange, R. D., Shivkumar, S., Chattoraj, A., & Haefner, R. M. (2023). Bayesian encoding and decoding as distinct perspectives on neural coding. *Nature Neuroscience, 26*(12), Article 12. https://doi.org/10.1038/s41593-023-01458-6.

Lathrop, R. G. (1967). Perceived variability. *Journal of Experimental Psychology, 73*, 498–502. https://doi.org/10.1037/h0024344.

Lau, H., & Rosenthal, D. (2011). Empirical support for higher-order theories of conscious awareness. *Trends in Cognitive Sciences, 15*(8), 365–373. https://doi.org/10.1016/j.tics.2011.05.009.

Lau, J. S., & Brady, T. F. (2018). Ensemble statistics accessed through proxies: Range heuristic and dependence on low-level properties in variability discrimination. *Journal of Vision, 18*(9), 3. https://doi.org/10.1167/18.9.3.

Lau, J. S.-H., Pashler, H., & Brady, T. F. (2021). Target templates in low target-distractor discriminability visual search have higher resolution, but the advantage they provide is short-lived. *Attention, Perception, & Psychophysics, 83*(4), 1435–1454. https://doi.org/10.3758/s13414-020-02213-w.

Li, A. Y., Liang, J. C., Lee, A. C. H., & Barense, M. D. (2020). The validated circular shape space: Quantifying the visual similarity of shape. *Journal of Experimental Psychology: General, 149*(5), 949. https://doi.org/10.1037/xge0000693.

Li, V., Herce Castañón, S., Solomon, J. A., Vandormael, H., & Summerfield, C. (2017). Robust averaging protects decisions from noise in neural computations. *PLoS Computational Biology, 13*(8), e1005723. https://doi.org/10.1371/journal.pcbi.1005723.

Li, V., Michael, E., Balaguer, J., Herce Castañón, S., & Summerfield, C. (2018). Gain control explains the effect of distraction in human perceptual, cognitive, and economic decision making. *Proceedings of the National Academy of Sciences, 115*(38), E8825–E8834. https://doi.org/10.1073/pnas.1805224115.

Ma, W. J. (2012). Organizing probabilistic models of perception. *Trends in Cognitive Sciences, 16*(10), 511–518. https://doi.org/10.1016/j.tics.2012.08.010.

Ma, W. J. (2019). Bayesian decision models: A primer. *Neuron, 104*(1), 164–175. https://doi.org/10.1016/j.neuron.2019.09.037.

Ma, W. J., Kording, K. P., & Goldreich, D. (2023). *Bayesian Models of Perception and Action: An Introduction*. The MIT Press.

Mack, A., & Rock, I. (1998). *Inattentional Blindness*. Cambridge, MA: The MIT Press.

Mack, A., Tang, B., Tuma, R., Kahn, S., & Rock, I. (1992). Perceptual organization and attention. *Cognitive Psychology, 24*, 475–501. https://doi.org/10.1016/0010-0285(92)90016-U.

Maljkovic, V., & Nakayama, K. (1994). Priming of pop-out: I. Role of features. *Memory & Cognition, 22*(6), 657–672.

Manassi, M., Liberman, A., Chaney, W., & Whitney, D. (2017). The perceived stability of scenes: Serial dependence in ensemble representations. *Scientific Reports, 7*(1), Article 1. https://doi.org/10.1038/s41598-017-02201-5.

Manassi, M., Lonchampt, S., Clarke, A., & Herzog, M. H. (2016). What crowding can tell us about object representations. *Journal of Vision, 16*(3), 35. https://doi.org/10.1167/16.3.35.

Manenti, G. L., Dizaji, A. S., & Schwiedrzik, C. M. (2023). Variability in training unlocks generalization in visual perceptual learning through invariant representations. *Current Biology, 33*(5), 817–826.e3. https://doi.org/10.1016/j.cub.2023.01.011.

Marr, D., Nishihara, H. K., & Brenner, S. (1978). Representation and recognition of the spatial organization of three-dimensional shapes. *Proceedings of the Royal Society of London. Series B. Biological Sciences, 200*(1140), 269–294. https://doi.org/10.1098/rspb.1978.0020.

Maule, J., & Franklin, A. (2015). Effects of ensemble complexity and perceptual similarity on rapid averaging of hue. *Journal of Vision, 15*(4), 6. https://doi.org/10.1167/15.4.6.

Maule, J., & Franklin, A. (2020). Adaptation to variance generalizes across visual domains. *Journal of Experimental Psychology. General, 149*(4), 662–675. https://doi.org/10.1037/xge0000678.

Mazyar, H., Berg, R. V. D., & Seilheimer, R. L. (2013). Independence is elusive: Set size effects on encoding precision in visual search. *Journal of Vision, 13* (2013), 1–14. https://doi.org/10.1167/13.5.8.

McKeefry, D. J., Watson, J. D. G., Frackowiak, R. S. J., Fong, K., & Zeki, S. (1997). The activity in human areas V1/V2, V3, and V5 during the perception of coherent and incoherent motion. *NeuroImage, 5*(1), 1–12. https://doi.org/10.1006/nimg.1996.0246.

Michael, E., de Gardelle, V., & Summerfield, C. (2014). Priming by the variability of visual information. *Proceedings of the National Academy of Sciences, 111*(21), 7873–7878. https://doi.org/10.1073/pnas.1308674111.

Mihali, A., & Ma, W. J. (2020). *The psychophysics of visual search with heterogeneous distractors* (p. 2020.08.10.244707). bioRxiv. https://doi.org/10.1101/2020.08.10.244707.

Mijalli, Y., Price, P. C., & Navarro, S. P. (2023). Spillover bias in social and nonsocial judgments of diversity and variability. *Psychonomic Bulletin & Review, 30*, 1829–1839. https://doi.org/10.3758/s13423-023-02259-5.

Mishkin, M., & Ungerleider, L. G. (1982). Contribution of striate inputs to the visuospatial functions of parieto-preoccipital cortex in monkeys. *Behavioural Brain Research, 6*(1), 57–77. https://doi.org/10.1016/0166-4328(82)90081-X.

Mitroff, S. R., & Simons, D. J. (2002). Changes are not localized before they are explicitly detected. *Visual Cognition, 9*(8), 937–968. https://doi.org/10.1080/13506280143000476.

Moore, C. M., & Egeth, H. (1997). Perception without attention: Evidence of grouping under conditions of inattention. *Journal of Experimental Psychology: Human Perception and Performance, 23*, 339–352. https://doi.org/10.1037/0096-1523.23.2.339.

Morgan, M. J., Chubb, C., & Solomon, J. A. (2008). A 'dipper' function for texture discrimination based on orientation variance. *Journal of Vision, 8*(11), 9–9. https://doi.org/10.1167/8.11.9.

Most, S. B., Simons, D. J., Scholl, B. J. et al. (2001). How not to be seen: The contribution of similarity and selective ignoring to sustained inattentional blindness. *Psychological Science, 12*(1), 9–17. https://doi.org/10.1111/1467-9280.00303.

Nagy, A. L., Neriani, K. E., & Young, T. L. (2005). Effects of target and distractor heterogeneity on search for a color target. *Vision Research*, *45*, 1885–1899. https://doi.org/10.1016/j.visres.2005.01.007.

Nakayama, K., Maljkovic, V., & Kristjánsson, Á. (2004). Short-term memory for the rapid deployment of visual attention. In Michael S. Gazzaniga (Ed.), *The Cognitive Neurosciences* (pp. 397–408). Cambridge, MA: MIT Press.

Navalpakkam, V., & Itti, L. (2007). Search goal tunes visual features optimally. *Neuron*, *53*(4), 605–617. https://doi.org/10.1016/j.neuron.2007.01.018.

Noe, A. (2002). Is the visual world a grand illusion? *Journal of Consciousness Studies*, *9*(5–6), 1–12.

Noe, A., Pessoa, L., & Thompson, E. (2000). Beyond the grand illusion: What change blindness really teaches us about vision. *Visual Cognition*, *7*(1–3), 93–106. https://doi.org/10.1080/135062800394702.

Norman, L. J., Heywood, C. A., & Kentridge, R. W. (2015). Direct encoding of orientation variance in the visual system. *Journal of Vision*, *15*, 1–14. https://doi.org/10.1167/15.4.3.

O'Regan, J. K. (1992). Solving the 'real' mysteries of visual perception: The world as an outside memory. *Canadian Journal of Psychology*, *46*(3), 461–488.

O'Regan, J. K., & Noë, A. (2001). A sensorimotor account of vision and visual consciousness. *Behavioral and Brain Sciences*, *24*(5), 939–973. https://doi.org/10.1017/S0140525X01000115.

O'Regan, J. K., Rensink, R. A., & Clark, J. J. (1999). Change-blindness as a result of 'mudsplashes'. *Nature*, *398*(6722), Article 6722. https://doi.org/10.1038/17953.

Oriet, C., & Brand, J. (2013). Size averaging of irrelevant stimuli cannot be prevented. *Vision Research*, *79*, 8–16. https://doi.org/10.1016/j.visres.2012.12.004.

Oriet, C., & Hozempa, K. (2016). Incidental statistical summary representation over time. *Journal of Vision*, *16*(3), 1–14. https://doi.org/10.1167/16.3.3.

Pascucci, D., Ceylan, G., & Kristjánsson, Á. (2022). Feature distribution learning by passive exposure. *Cognition*, *227*, 105211. https://doi.org/10.1016/j.cognition.2022.105211.

Pascucci, D., Tanrikulu, Ö. D., Ozkirli, A. et al. (2023). Serial dependence in visual perception: A review. *Journal of Vision*, *23*(1), 9. https://doi.org/10.1167/jov.23.1.9.

Payzan-LeNestour, E., Balleine, B. W., Berrada, T., & Pearson, J. (2016). Variance after-effects distort risk perception in humans. *Current Biology*, *26*(11), 1500–1504. https://doi.org/10.1016/j.cub.2016.04.023.

Pleskac, T. J., & Busemeyer, J. R. (2010). Two-stage dynamic signal detection: A theory of choice, decision time, and confidence. *Psychological Review, 117* (3), 864–901. https://doi.org/10.1037/a0019737.

Põder, E. (2012). On the rules of integration of crowded orientation signals. *I-Perception, 3,* 440–454. https://doi.org/10.1068/i0412.

Portilla, J., & Simoncelli, E. P. (2000). Parametric texture model based on joint statistics of complex wavelet coefficients. *International Journal of Computer Vision, 40*(1), 49–71. https://doi.org/10.1023/A:1026553619983.

Pouget, A., Beck, J. M., Ma, W. J., & Latham, P. E. (2013). Probabilistic brains: Knowns and unknowns. *Nature Neuroscience, 16*(9), 1170–1178. https://doi .org/10.1038/nn.3495.

Pouget, A., Dayan, P., & Zemel, R. S. (2000). Information processing with population codes. *Nature Reviews Neuroscience, 1*(2), 125–132. https://doi .org/10.1038/35039062.

Rafiei, M., Chetverikov, A., Hansmann-Roth, S., & Kristjánsson, Á. (2021a). You see what you look for: Targets and distractors in visual search can cause opposing serial dependencies. *Journal of Vision, 21*(10), 3. https://doi.org/ 10.1167/jov.21.10.3.

Rafiei, M., Hansmann-Roth, S., Whitney, D., Kristjánsson, Á., & Chetverikov, A. (2021b). Optimizing perception: Attended and ignored stimuli create opposing perceptual biases. *Attention, Perception, & Psychophysics, 83*(3), 1230–1239. https://doi.org/10.3758/s13414-020-02030-1.

Rahnev, D. (2017). *The case against full probability distributions in perceptual decision making.* bioRxiv. https://doi.org/10.1101/108944.

Rahnev, D., Block, N., Denison, R. N., & Jehee, J. (2021). *Is perception probabilistic? Clarifying the definitions.* PsyArXiv. https://doi.org/ 10.31234/osf.io/f8v5r.

Rahnev, D., & Denison, R. N. (2018). Suboptimality in perceptual decision making. *Behavioral and Brain Sciences, 41,* e223. https://doi.org/10.1017/ S0140525X18000936.

Ramgir, A., & Lamy, D. (2022). Does feature intertrial priming guide attention? The jury is still out. *Psychonomic Bulletin & Review, 29*(2), 369–393. https:// doi.org/10.3758/s13423-021-01997-8.

Rao, R. P. N., & Ballard, D. H. (1999). Predictive coding in the visual cortex: A functional interpretation of some extra-classical receptive-field effects. *Nature Neuroscience, 2*(1), Article 1. https://doi.org/10.1038/4580.

Rao, R. P., Olshausen, B. A., & Lewicki, M. S. (2002). *Probabilistic Models of the Brain: Perception and Neural Function.* Cambridge, MA: MIT Press.

Raviv, L., Lupyan, G., & Green, S. C. (2022). How variability shapes learning and generalization. *Trends in Cognitive Sciences*, *26*(6), 462–483. https://doi .org/10.1016/j.tics.2022.03.007.

Raviv, O., Ahissar, M., & Loewenstein, Y. (2012). How recent history affects perception: The normative approach and its heuristic approximation. *PLOS Computational Biology*, *8*(10), e1002731. https://doi.org/10.1371/journal .pcbi.1002731.

Rees, G., Friston, K. J., & Koch, C. (2000). A direct quantitative relationship between the functional properties of human and macaque V5. *Nature Neuroscience*, *3*(7), 716–723. https://doi.org/10.1038/76673.

Rensink, R. A. (2000). Visual search for change: A probe into the nature of attentional processing. *Visual Cognition*, *7*(1–3), 345–376. https://doi.org/ 10.1080/135062800394847.

Rensink, R. A., O'Regan, J. K., & Clark, J. J. (1997). To see or not to see: The need for attention to perceive changes in scenes. *Psychological Science*, *8*(5), 368–373. https://doi.org/10.1111/j.1467-9280.1997.tb00427.x.

Rosenholtz, R. (2001). Visual search for orientation among heterogeneous distractors: Experimental results and implications for signal-detection theory models of search. *Journal of Experimental Psychology: Human Perception and Performance*, *27*(4), 985–999. https://doi.org/10.1037//0096-1523.27.4.985.

Rosenholtz, R. (2016). Capabilities and limitations of peripheral vision. *Annual Review of Vision Science*, *2*(1), 437–457. https://doi.org/10.1146/annurev-vision-082114-035733.

Rosenholtz, R. (2020). Demystifying visual awareness: Peripheral encoding plus limited decision complexity resolve the paradox of rich visual experience and curious perceptual failures. *Attention, Perception, & Psychophysics*, *82*(3), 901–925. https://doi.org/10.3758/s13414-019-01968-1.

Rubin, N., Nakayama, K., & Shapley, R. (1997). Abrupt learning and retinal size specificity in illusory-contour perception. *Current Biology*, *7*, 461–467. https://doi.org/10.1016/S0960-9822(06)00217-X.

Saevarsson, S., Jóelsdóttir, S., Hjaltason, H., & Kristjánsson, Á. (2008). Repetition of distractor sets improves visual search performance in hemispatial neglect. *Neuropsychologia*, *46*(4), 1161–1169. https://doi.org/10.1016/ j.neuropsychologia.2007.10.020.

Sama, M. A., Srikanthan, D., Nestor, A., & Cant, J. S. (2021). Global and local interference effects in ensemble encoding are best explained by interactions between summary representations of the mean and the range. *Attention, Perception, & Psychophysics*, *83*(3), 1106–1128. https://doi.org/10.3758/ s13414-020-02224-7.

Schwartz, S., Maquet, P., & Frith, C. (2002). Neural correlates of perceptual learning: A functional MRI study of visual texture discrimination. *Proceedings of the National Academy of Sciences*, *99*(26), 17137–17142. https://doi.org/10.1073/pnas.242414599.

Scolari, M., & Serences, J. T. (2009). Adaptive allocation of attentional gain. *The Journal of Neuroscience*, *29*(38), 11933–11942. https://doi.org/10.1523/JNEUROSCI.5642-08.2009.

Seitz, A. R., & Watanabe, T. (2005). A unified model for perceptual learning. *Trends in Cognitive Sciences*, *9*(7), 329–334. https://doi.org/10.1016/j.tics.2005.05.010.

Semizer, Y., & Boduroglu, A. (2021). Variability leads to overestimation of mean summaries. *Attention, Perception, & Psychophysics*, *83*(3), 1129–1140. https://doi.org/10.3758/s13414-021-02269-2.

Seriès, P., & Seitz, A. R. (2013). Learning what to expect (in visual perception). *Frontiers in Human Neuroscience*, *7*(October), 668. https://doi.org/10.3389/fnhum.2013.00668.

Simons, D. J. (2000). Current approaches to change blindness. *Visual Cognition*, *7*(1–3), 1–15. https://doi.org/10.1080/135062800394658.

Simons, D. J., & Chabris, C. F. (1999). Gorillas in our midst: Sustained inattentional blindness for dynamic events. *Perception*, *28*(9), 1059–1074.

Solomon, J. A. (2010). Visual discrimination of orientation statistics in crowded and uncrowded arrays. *Journal of Vision*, *10*(14), 19. https://doi.org/10.1167/10.14.19.

Son, S., Lee, J., Kwon, O.-S., & Kim, Y.-J. (2021). *Effect of spatiotemporally changing environment on serial dependence in ensemble representations* (p. 2021.11.30.470662). bioRxiv. https://doi.org/10.1101/2021.11.30.470662.

Spence, M. L., Dux, P. E., & Arnold, D. H. (2016). Computations underlying confidence in visual perception. *Journal of Experimental Psychology: Human Perception and Performance*, *42*(5), 671–682. https://doi.org/10.1037/xhp0000179.

Spence, M. L., Mattingley, J. B., & Dux, P. E. (2018). Uncertainty information that is irrelevant for report impacts confidence judgments. *Journal of Experimental Psychology: Human Perception and Performance*, *44*(12), 1981–1994. https://doi.org/10.1037/xhp0000584.

Sperling, G. (1960). The information available in brief visual presentations. *Psychological Monographs: General and Applied*, *74*, 1–29. https://doi.org/10.1037/h0093759.

Suárez-Pinilla, M., Seth, A. K., & Roseboom, W. (2018). Serial dependence in the perception of visual variance. *Journal of Vision*, *18*(7), 1–24. https://doi.org/10.1167/18.7.4.

Sun, P., Chubb, C., Wright, C. E., & Sperling, G. (2018). High-capacity preconscious processing in concurrent groupings of colored dots. *Proceedings of the National Academy of Sciences, 115*(52), E12153–E12162. https://doi.org/10.1073/pnas.1814657115.

Tanrıkulu, Ö. D., Chetverikov, A., Hansmann-Roth, S., & Kristjánsson, Á. (2021a). What kind of empirical evidence is needed for probabilistic mental representations? An example from visual perception. *Cognition, 217,* 104903. https://doi.org/10.1016/j.cognition.2021.104903.

Tanrıkulu, Ö. D., Chetverikov, A., & Kristjánsson, Á. (2020). Encoding perceptual ensembles during visual search in peripheral vision. *Journal of Vision, 20*(8), 20. https://doi.org/10.1167/jov.20.8.20.

Tanrıkulu, Ö. D., Chetverikov, A., & Kristjánsson, Á. (2021b). Testing temporal integration of feature probability distributions using role-reversal effects in visual search. *Vision Research, 188*(July), 211–226. https://doi.org/10.1016/j.visres.2021.07.012.

Thornton, I. M., & Fernandez-Duque, D. (2000). An implicit measure of undetected change. *Spatial Vision, 14*(1), 21–44.

Tinsley, J. N., Molodtsov, M. I., Prevedel, R. et al. (2016). Direct detection of a single photon by humans. *Nature Communications, 7*(1), Article 1. https://doi.org/10.1038/ncomms12172.

Tiurina, N. A., Markov, Y. A., Choung, O.-H., Herzog, M. H., & Pascucci, D. (2022). Unlocking crowding by ensemble statistics. *Current Biology, 32*(22), P4975-4981.e3. https://doi.org/10.1016/j.cub.2022.10.003.

Tokita, M., Ueda, S., & Ishiguchi, A. (2016). Evidence for a global sampling process in extraction of summary statistics of item sizes in a set. *Frontiers in Psychology, 7*(MAY). https://doi.org/10.3389/fpsyg.2016.00711.

Tokita, M., Yang, Y., & Ishiguchi, A. (2020). Can we match the variance across different visual features? *CogSci2020.* https://cognitivesciencesociety.org/cogsci20/papers/0835/0835.pdf.

Tong, K., Ji, L., Chen, W., & Fu, X. (2015). Unstable mean context causes sensitivity loss and biased estimation of variability. *Journal of Vision, 15*(4), 15. https://doi.org/10.1167/15.4.15.

Tran, R., Vul, E., & Pashler, H. (2017). How effective is incidental learning of the shape of probability distributions? *Royal Society Open Science, 4*(8), 170270. https://doi.org/10.1098/rsos.170270.

Tsuchiya, N., Wilke, M., Frässle, S., & Lamme, V. A. F. (2015). No-report paradigms: Extracting the true neural correlates of consciousness. *Trends in Cognitive Sciences, 19*(12), 757–770. https://doi.org/10.1016/j.tics.2015.10.002.

Tyler, C. W. (2015). Peripheral color demo. *I-Perception, 6*(6), 2041669515613671. https://doi.org/10.1177/2041669515613671.

Ueda, S., Yakushijin, R., & Ishiguchi, A. (2023). Variance aftereffect within and between sensory modalities for visual and auditory domains. *Attention, Perception, & Psychophysics*. https://doi.org/10.3758/s13414-023-02705-5.

Usher, M., Bronfman, Z. Z., Talmor, S., Jacobson, H., & Eitam, B. (2018). Consciousness without report: Insights from summary statistics and inattention 'blindness'. *Philosophical Transactions of the Royal Society B: Biological Sciences*, *373*(1755), 20170354. https://doi.org/10.1098/rstb.2017.0354.

Utochkin, I. S. (2013). Visual search with negative slopes: The statistical power of numerosity guides attention. *Journal of Vision*, *13*(3), 1–14. https://doi.org/10.1167/13.3.18.

Utochkin, I. S., & Brady, T. F. (2020). Individual representations in visual working memory inherit ensemble properties. *Journal of Experimental Psychology: Human Perception and Performance*, *46*, 458–473. https://doi.org/10.1037/xhp0000727.

Utochkin, I. S., Choi, J., & Chong, S. C. (2023). A population response model of ensemble perception. *Psychological Review*, No Pagination Specified-No Pagination Specified. https://doi.org/10.1037/rev0000426.

Utochkin, I. S., & Tiurina, N. A. (2014). Parallel averaging of size is possible but range-limited: A reply to Marchant, Simons, and De Fockert. *Acta Psychologica*, *146*, 7–18. https://doi.org/10.1016/j.actpsy.2013.11.012.

Utochkin, I. S., & Yurevich, M. A. (2016). Similarity and heterogeneity effects in visual search are mediated by 'segmentability'. *Journal of Experimental Psychology: Human Perception and Performance*, *42*(7), 995–1007. https://doi.org/10.1037/xhp0000203.

van Bergen, R. S., & Jehee, J. F. M. (2019). Probabilistic representation in human visual cortex reflects uncertainty in serial decisions. *Journal of Neuroscience*, *39*(41), 8164–8176. https://doi.org/10.1523/JNEUROSCI.3212-18.2019.

van Bergen, R. S., Ma, W. J., Pratte, M. S., & Jehee, J. F. M. (2015). Sensory uncertainty decoded from visual cortex predicts behavior. *Nature Neuroscience*, *18*(12), 1728–1730. https://doi.org/10.1038/nn.4150.

Van de Cruys, S., Lemmens, L., Sapey-Triomphe, L. et al. (2021). Structural and contextual priors affect visual search in children with and without autism. *Autism Research*, *14*(7), 1484–1495. https://doi.org/10.1002/aur.2511.

van den Berg, R., & Ma, W. J. (2012). Robust averaging during perceptual judgment is not optimal. *Proceedings of the National Academy of Sciences*, *109*(13), E736–E736. https://doi.org/10.1073/pnas.1119078109.

Vilares, I., Howard, J. D., Fernandes, H. L., Gottfried, J. A., & Kording, K. P. (2012). Differential representations of prior and likelihood uncertainty in the human brain. *Current Biology, 22*(18), 1641–1648. https://doi.org/10.1016/j .cub.2012.07.010.

Vincent, B. T., Baddeley, R. J., Troscianko, T., & Gilchrist, I. D. (2009). Optimal feature integration in visual search. *Journal of Vision, 9*(5), 1–11. https://doi.org/10.1167/9.5.15.

Vul, E., Goodman, N., Griffiths, T. L., & Tenenbaum, J. B. (2014). One and done? Optimal decisions from very few samples. *Cognitive Science, 38*(4), 599–637. https://doi.org/10.1111/cogs.12101.

Walker, E. Y., Cotton, R. J., Ma, W. J., & Tolias, A. S. (2020). A neural basis of probabilistic computation in visual cortex. *Nature Neuroscience, 23*(1), 122–129. https://doi.org/10.1038/s41593-019-0554-5.

Walker, E. Y., Pohl, S., Denison, R. N., Barack, D. L., Lee, J., Block, N., Ma, W. J., & Meyniel, F. (2023). Studying the neural representations of uncertainty. *Nature Neuroscience,* 26(11), Article 11. https://doi.org/10.1038/s41593-023-01444-y.

Wallis, T. S. A., Bethge, M., & Wichmann, F. A. (2016). Testing models of peripheral encoding using metamerism in an oddity paradigm. *Journal of Vision, 16*(2), 1–30. https://doi.org/10.1167/16.2.4.

Wang, D., Kristjánsson, Á., & Nakayama, K. (2005). Efficient visual search without top-down or bottom-up guidance. *Perception & Psychophysics, 67*(2), 239–253. https://doi.org/10.3758/BF03206488.

Webster, M. A., Halen, K., Meyers, A. J., Winkler, P., & Werner, J. S. (2010). Colour appearance and compensation in the near periphery. *Proceedings of the Royal Society B: Biological Sciences, 277*(1689), 1817–1825. https://doi .org/10.1098/rspb.2009.1832.

Wei, X.-X., & Stocker, A. A. (2015). A Bayesian observer model constrained by efficient coding can explain 'anti-Bayesian' percepts. *Nature Neuroscience, 18*(10), 1509–1517. https://doi.org/10.1038/nn.4105.

Whitney, D., & Levi, D. M. (2011). Visual crowding: A fundamental limit on conscious perception and object recognition. *Trends in Cognitive Sciences, 15*(4), 160–168. https://doi.org/10.1016/j.tics.2011.02.005.

Whitney, D., & Yamanashi Leib, A. (2018). Ensemble perception. *Annual Review of Psychology, 69*(1), 105–129. https://doi.org/10.1146/annurev-psych-010416-044232.

Witkowski, P. P., & Geng, J. J. (2019). Learned feature variance is encoded in the target template and drives visual search. *Visual Cognition, 27*(5–8), 487–501. https://doi.org/10.1080/13506285.2019.1645779.

Witkowski, P. P., & Geng, J. J. (2022). Attentional priority is determined by predicted feature distributions. *Journal of Experimental Psychology: Human*

Perception and Performance, 48(11), 1201–1212. https://doi.org/10.1037/xhp0001041.

Witkowski, P. P., & Geng, J. J. (2023). Prefrontal cortex codes representations of target identity and feature uncertainty. *Journal of Neuroscience, 43*(50), 8769-8776. https://doi.org/10.1523/JNEUROSCI.1117-23.2023.

Witzel, C., & Gegenfurtner, K. R. (2013). Categorical sensitivity to color differences. *Journal of Vision, 13*(2013), 1–33. https://doi.org/10.1167/13.7.1.

Witzel, C., & Gegenfurtner, K. R. (2015). Categorical facilitation with equally discriminable colors. *Journal of Vision, 15*(8), 22. https://doi.org/10.1167/15.8.22.

Won, B.-Y., & Geng, J. J. (2018). Learned suppression for multiple distractors in visual search. *Journal of Experimental Psychology: Human Perception and Performance, 44*(7), 1128–1141. https://doi.org/10.1037/xhp0000521.

Woodman, G. F., Carlisle, N. B., & Reinhart, R. M. G. (2013). Where do we store the memory representations that guide attention? *Journal of Vision, 13* (3), 1–1. https://doi.org/10.1167/13.3.1.

Yoo, A. H., Acerbi, L., & Ma, W. J. (2021). Uncertainty is maintained and used in working memory. *Journal of Vision, 21*(8), 13. https://doi.org/10.1167/jov.21.8.13.

Yu, X., & Geng, J. J. (2019). The attentional template is shifted and asymmetrically sharpened by distractor context. *Journal of Experimental Psychology: Human Perception and Performance, 45*(3), 336–353. https://doi.org/10.1037/xhp0000609.

Zemel, R. S., Dayan, P., & Pouget, A. (1998). Probabilistic interpretation of population codes. *Neural Computation, 10*(2), 403–430. https://doi.org/10.1162/089976698300017818.

Zylberberg, A., Roelfsema, P. R., & Sigman, M. (2014). Variance misperception explains illusions of confidence in simple perceptual decisions. *Consciousness and Cognition, 27*(1), 246–253. https://doi.org/10.1016/j.concog.2014.05.012.

Acknowledgements

Large portions of the research described here were supported by a grant #173947–052 from the Icelandic Research Fund awarded to AC and AK. AK is furthermore supported by grants #207045–051 and #228366–051 from the Icelandic Research Fund and by the research fund of the University of Iceland. We are grateful to Alena Begler, Gianluca Campana, Sabrina Hansmann-Roth, Mohsen Rafiei, Ömer Dağlar Tanrıkulu, and many students who have contributed to the FDL studies and the development of the ideas described here. We also wish to thank Sang Chul Chong and two anonymous reviewers for very helpful comments on the manuscript.

Cambridge Elements ≡

Perception

James T. Enns
The University of British Columbia

Editor James T. Enns is Professor at the University of British Columbia, where he researches the interaction of perception, attention, emotion, and social factors. He has previously been Editor of the *Journal of Experimental Psychology: Human Perception and Performance* and an Associate Editor at *Psychological Science, Consciousness and Cognition, Attention Perception & Psychophysics*, and *Visual Cognition*.

Editorial Board

About the Series

The modern study of human perception includes event perception, bidirectional influences between perception and action, music, language, the integration of the senses, human action observation, and the important roles of emotion, motivation, and social factors. Each Element in the series combines authoritative literature reviews of foundational topics with forward-looking presentations of the recent developments on a given topic.

Cambridge Elements ≡

Perception

A full series listing is available at: www.cambridge.org/EPER

Milton Keynes UK
Ingram Content Group UK Ltd.
UKHW050657110324
439298UK00009B/53